"Dave, Norm, and Kate have found a simple and compelling way to pull together the study of leaders and leadership. We are using *The Leadership Code* with our high-potential leaders."

　　—Majed al-Romaithi, Executive Director, Abu Dhabi
　　　Investment Authority

"Comprehensive, focused, and immediately useful, *The Leadership Code* is an articulate and highly readable synthesis of current thinking on leadership—and a framework to apply such thinking in real-life situations. This should be recommended reading for all leaders and development professionals."

　　—Peter Goerke, Group Head of Human Resources, Zurich
　　　Financial Services

"Who knows if leaders are 'born' or 'made'? I know that leaders can become better. *The Leadership Code* shows them how! The best book on leading for the future that I have ever read—a wonderful combination of idealism and realism!"

　　—Marshall Goldsmith, author of the *Wall Street Journal*
　　　number-one bestseller *What Got You Here Won't Get
　　　You There*

"For current or aspiring leaders and those tasked with supporting and developing them, this book is a must-have. With inspiring leadership stories and wonderful frameworks and diagnostics, it provides a unique overview of what it takes to be a leader."

　　—Lynda Gratton, professor, London Business School, and
　　　author of *Hot Spots: Why Some Companies Buzz with Energy
　　　and Innovation—and Others Don't*

"A valuable guide through the thicket of leadership thinking, *The Leadership Code* summarizes what's core and critical to your leadership effectiveness."

—Herminia Ibarra, Cora Chaired Professor in Leadership and Learning, INSEAD, and Faculty Director, INSEAD Leadership Initiative

"The concepts of leadership brand and leadership code are both developmental and useful. We have used these ideas at Ketchum to focus and define our leadership to better serve both our clients and colleagues. I heartily endorse this book as a useful guide to improving and strengthening your organization's leadership."

—Ray Kotcher, CEO, Ketchum

"Not just another book on leadership, but a truly useful guide to what leaders can and should do. Integrates the research on leadership and provides a what-to-do list of actions and useful examples."

—Ed Lawler, professor, Marshall School of Business, University of Southern California, and author of *Talent: Making People your Competitive Advantage*

"A hard-hitting, back-to-basics reminder of leadership fundamentals that are all too readily forgotten in today's task-driven culture. The commonsense approach of *The Leadership Code* provides some practical tools to guide and measure success. The five rules clearly define the critical pathway from creating strategy to delivering results, engaging both employees and customers along the way. A must for aspiring leaders and managers who value their development and effectiveness."

—Tony McCarthy, Director, People and Organisational Effectiveness, British Airways

"Going beyond theories, *The Leadership Code* brings different ideas together under a single framework to develop organizational capabilities for business success. Refreshing and inspiring real-world examples make this book a valuable how-to guide for today's leaders. Simply put, it's value-added and it makes a difference."

—Randy McDonald, Senior Vice President, Human
Resources, IBM

"In an environment where everyone is claiming to have the 'magic pill' for effective leadership, Ulrich, Smallwood, and Sweetman present an innovative approach that speaks for itself. A thoughtful spin on traditional content, the authors equip readers with a personalized, pragmatic rulebook that simplifies a rather dense body of research and enables managers in any field to enrich their leadership skills. As dynamic as it is telling, *The Leadership Code* integrates theory, assessment tools, and practical examples in a way that encourages both introspection and incremental development."

—Lynne Oldham, Managing Director, Head of HR North
America, BNP Paribas

"Is leadership an art or a science? Is leadership a 'hard' or 'soft' discipline? The great contribution of this book is that it dismisses these tired dichotomies and proposes an integrated and actionable theory of leadership based on the art and the science and the importance of *both* the soft and hard skills that are necessary to lead. It promises to move the field forward in a powerful and helpful way."

—Fran Sussner Rodgers, Chair of WFD and recipient of the
Ernst & Young/Merrill Lynch Entrepreneur of the Year
award

"Simple yet complex, conceptual and practical, *The Leadership Code* is a book designed to drive action and in that sense it a must for all managers and leaders. It is a great distillation of practical ideas, insights, and activities designed to grow great leaders at all levels in organizations."

　　—Neil Roden, Group Director, Human Resources, Royal Bank of Scotland

"An excellent, thoughtful read that extends the knowledge base of leadership by providing easy to understand and apply concepts and frameworks. Importantly, this book differentiates itself in an overstudied field by driving the reader to the pure essence of leadership and showing how each one of us, regardless of level or position, can become more personally proficient at leading."

　　—Dennis W. Shuler, Chief Human Resources Officer, The Walt Disney Company.

"Finally—a practical, comprehensive framework about what leaders do and why they do it. This book rises like Everest above all other leadership books. *The Leadership Code* is destined to become as fundamentally important to leadership as Newton's laws are to physics or Magellan's circumnavigation was to geography."

　　—Dave Weidman, CEO, Celanese Corporation

THE
LEADERSHIP
CODE

THE LEADERSHIP CODE

Five Rules to Lead By

Dave Ulrich, Norm Smallwood,
Kate Sweetman

HARVARD BUSINESS PRESS

Boston, Massachusetts

No part of this publication may be reproduced, stored in or intro-
duced into a retrieval system, or transmitted, in any form, or by any
means (electronic, mechanical, photocopying, recording, or otherwise), without the prior permission of the publisher. Requests for
permission should be directed to permissions@hbsp.harvard.edu,
or mailed to Permissions, Harvard Business School Publishing,
60 Harvard Way, Boston, Massachusetts 02163.

ISBN 978-1-4221-1901-3
Library of Congress Cataloging-in-Publication Data

Ulrich, Dave, 1953-
    The new leadership code : five rules to lead by / by Dave Ulrich,
Norm Smallwood, Kate Sweetman.
      p. cm.
    ISBN 1-4221-1901-7
    1. Leadership.   I. Smallwood, W. Norman.   II. Sweetman, Kate.
III. Title.
    HD57.7.U444 2008
    658.4'092—dc22

                                                  2008029732

The paper used in this publication meets the requirements of the
American National Standard for Permanence of Paper for Publications
and Documents in Libraries and Archives Z39.48-1992.

To our fathers, who gave us our code:

Richard Ulrich, Ken Smallwood,

and Richard Sweetman

Contents

Acknowledgments

If it takes a village to raise a child, then it takes a city to write a book. We hope here that we acknowledge everyone who has contributed in so many ways to this book from its inception to its final realization.

We owe special thanks to Harvard Business Press for their ongoing support, especially Melinda Merino, who is our ever-gracious and insightful editor.

We owe a special thanks to Bob Eichinger, who has consistently provoked and encouraged us.

We also owe a special thanks to Omar Kader, who gave us invaluable feedback as we wrote various chapters of this manuscript, and Dean Weatherford, who provided new perspectives and encouragement.

Thanks to those who have attended our workshops, where we test our ideas and learn from their questions and insights.

Deep gratitude to all the folks we interviewed . . . they are in the book already, but we acknowledge them here as well because without them there would be no leadership code and no book. These generous thought leaders include Jim Bolt (working on leadership development efforts); Richard Boyatzis (working on the competency models and resonant leadership); Jay Conger (working on leadership skills as aligned to strategy); Marc Effron (working on large studies of global leaders); Bob Fulmer (working on leadership skills); Marshall Goldsmith (working on global leadership skills and how to develop those skills); Gary Hamel (working on leadership as it relates to strategy); Linda Hill (working on how managers become leaders and leadership in emerging economies); Jon Katzenbach (working on leaders from within the organization); Jim Kouzes (working on how leaders build credibility); Morgan McCall (representing the Center for Creative Leadership); Barry Posner (working on how leaders build credibility); Paul Thompson (working on current development styles) and Jack Zenger and Joe Folkman (working on how leaders deliver results and become extraordinary).

Thanks, of course, to our valued colleagues at RBL past and present, without whom this work would not be possible: Jon Younger, Wayne Brockbank, Judy Seegmiller, Barbara Ferre, Ginger Bitter, Loretta Allen, Ernesto Uscher

Justin Allen, Dave Hanna, Allan Freed, Bonner Ritchie, Gene Dalton, Erin Wilson Burns, Tim Kapp, Justin Britton, Meggan Pingree, David Gilliland, and Mark Nyman.

And to the host of other people who helped us to work through these ideas, and who provided facts and figures where we had none: Kara Helander, Robert Burnside, and Robin Athey.

Very large thanks to our families, who tolerate our writing obsession: Wendy Ulrich, Tricia Smallwood, and Alexis "Yoshi" Belash and Kate's very patient daughters Isabel and Ali. And, of course, Kate's mother, Mary Sweetman, who instilled her own strong code.

Defining
Leadership Code

NO ONE DISPUTES that leadership matters. We recognize good leadership firsthand when a leader we admire inspires, excites, engages, or even leaves us. Beyond our personal awareness, research has shown that the quality of leadership helps meet the expectations of investors, customers, and employees. While we can stipulate that leadership matters and that we know it when we encounter it, it is much more difficult to find the elusive answer to the simple question, "What makes an effective leader?" In study after study about what CEOs worry about, a chronically important topic is how to develop the next generation of effective leaders.

This book attempts to do the improbable, if not the impossible. In a brief and clear way, we want to synthesize large numbers of frameworks, tools, processes, and studies of leadership to identify the essential rules that govern what all great leaders do. The challenge of synthesizing this amorphous and enormous body of knowledge is not easy, but it is important. Defining the essential rules of leadership serves two purposes: we want to help leaders be better leaders themselves and simultaneously help those charged with building better leadership in their organizations.

Being an effective leader starts with the self. If you want to build leadership in your company, you need to model what you want others to know and do. When you can clearly declare what makes an effective leader and then model that behavior, your employees will have clear expectations of what they should know and do, your customers will be delighted to do business with you, investors will have more confidence in the intangible value of your company, and you can make wise investments in finding and developing future leaders.

Being an effective leader requires that you help others to lead. Leaders succeed by enabling others to do the right work right. Modeling the rules of leadership ensures that you lead well, but helping others master those rules guarantees future success. When we know and follow the leadership rules, we lead well; when we help others learn and follow those rules, we expand leadership from a personal ability into an organization capability.

The leadership rules we propose in this work offer a unified way of *thinking about* being a better leader and *being* a better leader. We have examined the broad field, talked in depth with the smartest leadership people we know, and passed all that information through the screen of our own collective hundred years of experience in the field. Through that process, we have discovered and validated what we now know to be the five essential rules all excellent leaders must follow. Since these rules form the basis for all good leaders just as our genetic code determines our elemental core as people, we call it the *leadership code*.

This leadership code, like any other code, provides both structure and guidance, and helps you know not only what to do to be a better individual leader, but also how to build better leadership capability. Some leaders seem born to the code, others need to learn it, but it is the sine qua non of effective leadership. The code also avoids the trap of emphasizing one element of leadership over others. For example, when we ask thoughtful participants in programs where we teach, "What makes an effective leader?" we often get a long list of outstanding ideas. Some focus on the importance of having a vision for the future; others on executing in the present; others on personal charisma or character; others on engaging people; and others on building long-term organizations. Shopping lists of leadership attributes are useful, but they may distort the fundamentals of effective leadership. Purchasing food on a whim from a last-minute shopping list may not lead to healthy eating across all four food groups. The four food groups offer a decision architecture that ensures balance in purchasing food and healthy eating—if the framework is followed. Having a leadership code that captures the entire domain of what makes an effective leader helps leaders avoid fads and quick fixes that offer the illusion of true leadership but, like snack foods, fail to sustain success.

So, we do not disagree with most of the current hot topics that entice leaders. We agree that leaders need to have innovative (e.g., blue ocean) strategies, forge long-term relationships with customers, innovate, execute, build high-performing teams, ensure accountability, manage people, communicate, engage others, create workforce plans, exercise judgment, have emotional intelligence, and possess an honorable character. Any one of these topics deserves (and has received) extensive research, thinking, and practice. What we offer in this book is a synthesis of these ideas, a way to cover the landscape of leadership so that we see the whole of what makes an effective leader, not just one of the parts.

We characterize the leadership code as a set of five rules. Rules lay out how a game is played; they suggest the basic elements of any endeavor. Knowing the rules enables you to adapt your behavior and succeed. In sports, rules determine the type of talent and game plan that teams adopt. In writing, rules shape the use of language to communicate. In politics, rules often establish who wins and loses. In driving, rules ensure safety and fluidity. In leadership, rules resolve what makes an effective leader.

HOW WE DISCOVERED THE LEADERSHIP CODE

In our efforts to arrive at the core rules of leadership, we decided to rely not only on our experiences, but also to mine a vast, well-researched body of knowledge painstakingly accumulated by multiple generations of leadership experts and organizational behavior theorists. In a brief and clear way, we wanted to synthesize the existing frameworks, tools, processes, and studies of leadership to define the rules that all great leaders follow. To streamline our efforts, we "socially networked" our way through the ranks of many of the most recognized leaders in the field of leadership today and did considerable reading, thinking, debating, and writing ourselves. Our goal: to identify an underlying framework of knowledge, skills, and values common to all effective leaders.

In our work, we found that the state of the art of leadership has evolved over time, each new stage building at least in part on its predecessors. A brief history of modern attempts to understand leadership may help you to put this conclusion in perspective. Interestingly, as we organized this history, we realized that the six key questions that any journalist asks to uncover the full story have been asked and thoroughly investigated over the past few decades: who, what, when, where, why, and how. To these questions was added a seventh: for whom?

- *Physical traits: Who* is a leader? Remember when all leaders were supposed to be tall and authoritative, with a firm handshake and a steady gaze? Leadership theorists sought a core set of leadership traits according to height, gender, heritage, and speaking style—to no avail. Successful leaders could have a variety of backgrounds as well as physical and personality traits.

- *Style: How* do you behave as a leader? "Take care" or "take charge"? Leadership theorists sought to characterize a leader by style, often a trade-off between people and task. Generally, leaders exhibited a preferred style, but the best leaders could be both soft and hard, caring about people and managing tasks. Leaders were given number rankings (1–9; 9–1; 9–9) to capture their tendency to focus on people or tasks.

- *Situation: When* and *where* do you focus on the person or the task? At this stage, the answer to the leadership question is: "It depends." Leadership theorists realized that the appropriate leadership style depended on understanding the particulars of the situation.

- *Competencies: What* exactly do leaders know and do? Leadership theorists attempted to identify the core competencies, or knowledge, skills, and values of successful leaders.[1] Competencies were identified by what leaders said and did and were often tailored to not only the situation but to the business strategy. The world is awash in competency models.

- *Results: Why* does leadership matter? More recently, the focus has shifted to the truth that without results, competencies don't matter.[2] Leadership is about getting the right results in the right way. Leaders who can achieve a balanced scorecard of employee, customer, investor, and organization results will more likely succeed.

- *Brand: For whom* are you leading? Students of leadership now realize that leadership is linking the external identity of the firm (its brand) with the internal culture. Leaders ensure that the behaviors of employees reflect the leadership brand.

We believe it is time to synthesize decades of empirical research and theorizing about leadership. Faced with half a million books on leaders and leadership, we turned to recognized experts in the field who had already spent years sifting through the evidence and developing their own theories. These thought leaders had each published a theory of leadership based on a long history of leadership research and empirical assessment of what makes effective leadership. Collectively, they have written over fifty books on leadership and performed well over 2 million leadership 360s. They are the thought leaders of this field.[3]

In our discussions with them, as well as our reading and analysis, we constantly returned to two basic sets of questions:

1. What percent of effective leadership is basically the same? Are there some common rules that any leader anywhere must master? Is there a recognizeable leadership code?

2. If there are common rules that all leaders must master, what are they?

The questions are simple, but the answers are elusive. In answering the first questions, experts varied—estimating that somewhere in the range of 50 to 85 percent of leadership characteristics were shared across all effective leaders. The range is fairly broad, to be sure, but blessedly consistent. As one of our interviews put it: "I think . . . that 85 percent of the competencies in various competency models appear to be the same. I think we have a relatively good handle on the necessary competencies for a leader to possess in order to be effective." Then the expert added something of equally great significance: "But there are some other variables that competency models do not account for. [Among] the variables that I think we don't account for include . . . the leader's personal situation (family pressures, economics, competition, social, etc.); [and] internal influences, such as health, energy, vitality, resilience; the intensity of effort the individual is willing to put forth, ambition and drive, willingness to sacrifice."[4]

Answers like these encouraged us to pursue developing a framework. From the body of interviews we conducted, we concluded that 60 to 70 percent of leadership effectiveness would be contained in the leadership code if we could crack it. Synthesizing the data, the interviews, and our own research and experience, we saw a pattern that organizes the leadership code into a single framework that we believe is accurate, logical, and useful.

An analogy guided our thinking. How different is the hybrid Toyota Prius from the Ford F-150 truck? If you are like most people, you likely view the two vehicles as being very different from each other. Perhaps even opposites. The eco-friendly Prius appeals to people interested in shrinking their personal carbon footprint while still getting about. The massive and sturdy F-150, on the other hand, is a perfect vehicle for people who equate driving with personal freedom and who highly value the pure pleasure of owning the open road. You may love to drive one and not want to be caught dead in the other, believing them to be very different species.

But are they really? Underneath the obvious external characteristics, they share more in common than they differ. First of all, they are both forms of individual (versus mass) transportation. They both get you where you need to go. They each do that by sharing an important set of core elements: drive train, crankshaft, engine, brakes, wipers, blades, and batteries. In fact, when you add it up, the degree to which any two cars share fundamental similarities is much greater than their differences.

As we listened to leadership experts, we felt that the same logic would apply. Does an effective leader at, say,

Starbucks or Whole Foods in any way resemble an effective leader at ExxonMobil? Does an effective leader in a bootstrapping NGO in any way resemble an effective leader at the famously bureaucratic United Nations? Does an effective leader in an emerging market resemble an effective leader in a mature market? Does an effective leader in organized crime in any way resemble an effective leader in organized religion? Does an effective leader in a Swiss pharmaceutical company share any underlying characteristics with an effective leader in MoveOn.org? Does an effective leader at Nokia resemble an effective leader at Verizon?

Consider the following tale of two brothers. In the city of Boston, two brothers grew up together in the same household—Billy Bulger and Whitey Bulger. They definitely share a leadership gene, or a leadership learning environment, or both. However, Billy grew up to be the head of the university system for the state of Massachusetts, while Whitey grew up to be the very powerful and notorious head of the local Irish mafia. Both are leaders, each with his talents quite differently applied, and each could be called "successful" in his own pursuit (until that informant . . .).

As we worked with these leadership experts and reviewed the extensive work on leadership, we concluded that leadership comprises two principle parts: one part the *leadership code* and the other the *differentiators*. The code represents about 60 to 70 percent of what makes an effective leader. It represents the basics, the fundamentals, or the essentials of leadership. The differentiators may vary by firm strategy and vision and by individual job requirements. Mastering the code becomes the foundation on which effective leadership is established.

LEADERSHIP CODE: TIME, FOCUS, AND SELF

Based on our observations and inputs from the thought leaders, we suggest that leadership code maps against two dimensions, time and attention, and is supported by the strength of the individual leader. Why *time*? Because effective leaders are able to think and act both in the short term and for the long term. Effective leaders project into the future and define a context in which their organization and their people will succeed. Depending on the need, that projection may take the form of a vision, intent, purpose, mission, strategy, goal, objective, or plan. In all of these cases, leaders create a credible and hopeful image of a future for everyone who needs to invest financially, intellectually, physically, or emotionally in the organization, from financial markets to shareholders to customers to employees to potential hires. They also connect the future to the present by turning aspirations into actions.

What do we mean by *attention*? Effective leaders gauge when their focus needs to be on architecting the organization and its capabilities, and when it needs to shift to individuals and their abilities. They are also able to connect the two to each other. Sometimes leaders focus on individual talent and surround themselves with gifted individual contributors. But all-star teams would not often beat a high-performing team, and leaders need to meld individual talents into successful organization capabilities.

In terms of *self*, leaders must model what they want others to master. Leadership of others ultimately begins with the self. Individuals who govern themselves will be more able to lead others. There is a vast array of self-leadership requirements, which we called *personal proficiency* because an individual leader needs to become highly proficient in these personal requirements. Without personal proficiency, it is not possible to keep the other dimensions in balance. The juggling act is simply too difficult for someone who is not personally strong, aware, and centered.

In an effort to create a useful visual, we have mapped out two dimensions (time and focus) and placed what we are calling personal proficiency (self-management) at the center as an underlying support for the other two. Figure 1-1

FIGURE 1-1

The leadership code

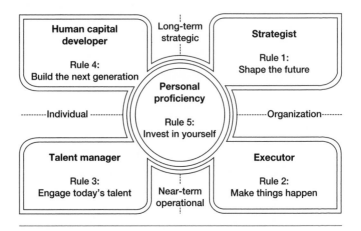

synthesizes the leadership code and captures the five rules of leadership.

Rule 1: Shape the Future. This rule is embodied in the *strategist* dimension of the leader. Strategists answer the question, "Where are we going?" and make sure that those around them understand the direction as well. They not only envision, but can create a future. As practical futurists, they figure out where the organization needs to go to succeed, they test these ideas pragmatically against current resources (money, people, organizational capabilities), and they work with others to figure out how to get from the present to the desired future. Strategists have a point of view about the future and are able to position their organization to create and respond to that future. The rules for strategists are about creating, defining, and delivering principles of what can be.

Rule 2: Make Things Happen. Turn what you know into what you do. The *executor* dimension of the leader focuses on the question, "How will we make sure we get to where we are going?" Executors translate strategy into action. Executors understand how to make change happen, to assign accountability, to know which key decisions to take and which to delegate, and to make sure that teams work well together. They keep promises to multiple stakeholders. Executors make things happen, and put the systems in place for others to do the same. The rules for executors revolve around disciplines for getting things done.

Rule 3: Engage Today's Talent. Leaders who optimize talent today answer the question, "Who goes with us on our business journey?" *Talent managers* know how to identify, build, and engage talent to get results *now*. Talent managers identify what skills are required, draw talent to their organizations, develop people, engage them, and ensure that employees turn in their best efforts. Talent managers generate intense personal, professional, and organizational loyalty. The rules for talent managers center around resolutions that help people develop themselves for the good of the organization.

Rule 4: Build the Next Generation. Leaders who are *human capital developers* answer the question, "Who stays and sustains the organization for the next generation?" Talent managers ensure shorter-term results through people, while human capital developers ensure that the organization has the longer-term competencies required for future strategic success. Just as good parents invest in helping their children succeed, human capital developers help future leaders to be successful. Human capital developers throughout the organization build a workforce plan focused on future talent, understand how to develop the future talent, and help employees see their future careers within the company. Human capital developers ensure that the organization will outlive any single individual. Human capital developers install rules that demonstrate a pledge to building the next generation of talent.

We found in our work that most individuals have predispositions to one of these four roles. Some enjoy living in the abstract and future world of strategy; others in the concrete and actionable execution space; others are comfortable with the social setting required of talent; and others are gifted at developing future talent. We also found that as leaders move up the organization into more senior roles, they need to expand out from their predisposition and learn to successfully master the rules to play all four roles. This book offers specific actions that leaders can master in each of the four roles so that even if the role does not come naturally, it can be learned.

Rule 5: Invest in Yourself. At the heart of the leadership code—literally and figuratively—is *personal proficiency*. Effective leaders cannot be reduced to what they know and do. Who they are as human beings has everything to do with how much they can accomplish with and through other people. To distinguish between what one does— even with excellence—and who one is, consider the following passage from Matthieu Ricard in his book *Happiness*:

> *The striking individuals with whom I'd crossed paths each had his or her own special genius. I'd have liked to play piano like Glenn Gould, or chess like Bobby Fischer, to have Baudelaire's poetic gift, but I did not feel inspired to become what they were at the human level. Despite their artistic, scientific, and intellectual qualities, when it came to altruism, openness to the world, resolve, and joie de vivre, their ability was neither better nor worse than that of any of us . . . I was inspired through my readings of great figures like Martin Luther King, Jr.,*

and Mohandas Gandhi, who by sheer strength of their
human qualities were able to inspire others to change
their way of being.[5]

Leaders are learners: from success, failure, assignments, books, classes, people, and life itself. Passionate about their beliefs and interests, they expend enormous personal energy and attention on whatever matters to them. Effective leaders inspire loyalty and goodwill in others because they themselves act with integrity and trust. Decisive and impassioned, they are capable of bold and courageous moves. Confident in their ability to deal with situations as they arise, they can tolerate ambiguity. Think of the steadfastness of Winston Churchill or Nelson Mandela or Aung San Suu Kyi persevering in the face of certain danger, and probable disaster. Leaders who demonstrate personal proficiency follow rules about developing and increasing personal insight so that they model the change they want to see in others.

In the last few years, we have worked with these five rules of leadership. As a result, we can make some summary observations.

- All leaders must excel at personal proficiency. Without the foundation of trust and credibility, you cannot ask others to follow you. While individuals may have different styles (introvert versus extrovert, intuitive versus sensing, etc.), any individual leader must be seen as having personal proficiency to engage followers.

- All leaders must have one towering strength. Most successful leaders excel in at least one of the other four roles. Most are personally predisposed to one of the four areas. These are the signature strengths of your leaders.

- All leaders must be at least average in their "weaker" leadership domains.

- The higher up the organization that the leader rises, the more he or she needs to develop excellence in more than one of the four domains.

LEADERSHIP CODE: MAKING IT REAL FOR YOU AND YOUR ORGANIZATION

If you want to be a better leader or build more effective leadership in your organization, you need to learn these five rules of leadership. As an individual leader, some of these rules will come naturally; some will have to be learned. Each person's leadership will look and feel somewhat different, based on personality as well as more external circumstances (position, job level, industry, company culture). That said, every leader must master the fundamentals. Without owning these basics, an individual cannot lead and CEOs cannot invest in future leaders because they won't know what they are looking for.

You may ask yourself which of the five rules come more naturally to you. Where do you enjoy spending time? What work comes more easily? What work energizes you? Knowing your predisposition enables you to develop a signature leadership strength. It also focuses your attention on what you must learn to progress in becoming a more effective leader. If you are strong as a strategist, you may need to pay particular attention to the rules for talent management, execution, and human capital development. A simple personal exercise is to take the abbreviated leadership code survey find out your predispositions (assessment 1-1). To be more informed, you may want to solicit feedback from others on how they see you and compare yourself with others' national scores.

At a company level, we have used the leadership code template to track if the organization has the right competency model. Often when we place a company's seven to twelve competencies into the five rules, we find that the model is unbalanced. One company identified twelve competencies it wanted its leaders to demonstrate, then

ASSESSMENT 1-1

Leadership code self-assessment

For the first four domains of the leadership code, or the action domains, identify which domain had the highest average score. This is your area of strength in the leadership code.

If you scored 3 or lower on any of the items in the personal proficiency domain, identify how you might build your competency in this area to ensure sustained leadership effectiveness.

Scale: 1 = Low ◄ - - ► 10 = High

Strategist

I have a point of view about the future 1 2 3 4 5 6 7 8 9 10

I create a customercentric view of strategy 1 2 3 4 5 6 7 8 9 10

I engage my organization in developing strategy 1 2 3 4 5 6 7 8 9 10

I create strategic traction in my organization 1 2 3 4 5 6 7 8 9 10

(Strategist Total) _____ ÷ 4 = _____

Executor

I make change happen 1 2 3 4 5 6 7 8 9 10

I follow a decision protocol 1 2 3 4 5 6 7 8 9 10

I ensure accountability 1 2 3 4 5 6 7 8 9 10

I build teams 1 2 3 4 5 6 7 8 9 10

I ensure technical proficiency 1 2 3 4 5 6 7 8 9 10

(Executor Total)_____ ÷ 5 = _____

Talent manager

I communicate effectively 1 2 3 4 5 6 7 8 9 10

I create aligned direction 1 2 3 4 5 6 7 8 9 10

I strengthen competency in my organization 1 2 3 4 5 6 7 8 9 10

I resource to cope with demands 1 2 3 4 5 6 7 8 9 10

I create a positive work environment 1 2 3 4 5 6 7 8 9 10

(Talent Manager Total)_____ ÷ 5 = _____

Human capital developer

I map the workforce 1 2 3 4 5 6 7 8 9 10

I link firm and employee brand 1 2 3 4 5 6 7 8 9 10

I help people manage their careers 1 2 3 4 5 6 7 8 9 10

I find and develop next-generation talent 1 2 3 4 5 6 7 8 9 10

I encourage networks and relationships in the organization .. 1 2 3 4 5 6 7 8 9 10

(Human Capital Developer Total)____ ÷ 5 = ____

Personal proficiency

I practice clear thinking ....….... 1 2 3 4 5 6 7 8 9 10

I know myself 1 2 3 4 5 6 7 8 9 10

I tolerate stress ....…. 1 2 3 4 5 6 7 8 9 10

I demonstrate learning agility ....…. 1 2 3 4 5 6 7 8 9 10

I model character and integrity ....…. 1 2 3 4 5 6 7 8 9 10

I take care of myself ....….... 1 2 3 4 5 6 7 8 9 10

I have personal energy and passion ....…..... 1 2 3 4 5 6 7 8 9 10

(Personal Proficiency Total)____ ÷ 7 = ____

built a leadership 360, training, and compensation systems to encourage these twelve competencies. When we matched these competencies to the five rules, eleven of the twelve were in personal proficiency. The company had a flawed model of the basics of leadership. Even if its leaders excelled at mastering their proposed competencies, they would not be doing all the basics well. The company was eating only from one food group and wondering why it wasn't healthy. A simple organization exercise is to match your organization's competency model against the five rules we have suggested. Do you want leaders who are effective in all five areas?

The purpose of this book is to synthesize what we know about the basics of leadership so that we can each understand how to be and build better leaders. Leadership can be developed through education, experience, mentoring, coaching, job assignment, and leaders teaching leaders. There is no magic bullet. The essential thing is to know what leadership dimensions need to be developed, and then develop them. By defining the basic rules of leadership, you can examine your own leadership style *and* organize effective leadership development efforts to build future leaders.

If you want to be a better leader or build more effective leadership in your organization, you need to master these rules. Some of these characteristics will come naturally; some will have to be learned. Each person's leadership will look and feel somewhat different based on personality as well as more external circumstances (position, job level, industry, company culture). That said, every leader must master the fundamentals. Without owning these basics, an individual cannot lead and leaders cannot invest in future leaders—because they won't know what they are looking for.

Go to www.leadershipcodebook.com for a brief video lesson from Dave Ulrich that will help you to interpret the results of the short leadership code self-assessment tool in assessment 1-1. He will also introduce you to our leadership code premium tools collection, including a full-length leadership code assessment in both self-assessment and 360 forms.

Rule 1

Shape the Future

To shape the future, be a *strategist*:

1. Stay curious and develop a point of view about your own future.
2. Invite your savviest outsiders inside.
3. Engage the organization—no "one" knows enough.
4. Create strategic traction within the organization.

STRATEGY IS BEING CLEAR about where you want to go. That strategic end point may be defending a strong and lucrative niche (think here of Harvard University or IBM); or setting speed records in getting new products and services to market (how many new businesses and products has Google launched?); or perfecting a set of capabilities that combine in ways that that no competitor could hope to replicate (consider the winning selection of capabilities behind any Disney theme park in the world). The language may differ—mission, vision, goals, strategies, objectives, outcomes, values, and so forth—but any leader's intention is to create a future that is even more attractive than the present by occupying a strategic position that no one else can touch.

Strategists combine vision and analytics. They envision a future state that creates or responds to opportunities. They specify rigorous financial, customer, technology, and organization analytics to build a path to reach the future state. To be both visionary and analytical, strategic leaders must clearly understand their organization's current core competencies (technical skills like creating space-age adhesives, state-of-the-art engines, world-class logistics support, or great consumer design), organization capabilities (the company's culture and ways of doing things, like collaborating across boundaries, managing talent, or knowing how to get new products to market fast), financial resources, and technology. Effective strategists distinguish themselves by enabling their organizations to harness these strengths in ways that no one else does or can hope to do realistically.

If you are going to be a good strategist, you need to avoid common pitfalls of creating strategy:

- Don't leave strategy as a set of aspirational edicts that proclaim a future without specifics to sustain the ideas. Mission and visions not rooted in reality create more cynicism than confidence. One senior leadership team we knew spent months drafting their mission, vision, values, and other noble statements. When they sent these out with a DVD and self-paced workshop to over fifty thousand employees, they expected great acclaim; what they received instead was what we called SPOTS (strategic plans on top shelf). Employees read the rhetoric, but did not see the action.

- Don't claim that merely projecting today's numbers into the future is a strategy. Pages of analytics about financial results and projections, current and future customer and employee trends, and technology and manufacturing processes may mask the lack of a real strategy. We worked with a senior team that had spent two days looking first at financial and then at extensive customer data; on day three we asked a simple question: "In twenty words or less, what is your strategy?" We were not surprised that the individuals each had a unique, not shared, answer to this simple question of where they wanted to go. Their analytics did not add up to a shared direction.

- Don't just follow industry leaders; instead, try to leapfrog them to a unique position in your industry. Benchmarking is useful for learning what the best do—so that you can do it better or differently.

- Don't let past success dictate your future strategic choices; past success may not predict the future as much as you may think. The liability of success is that what has worked may lead you to do the wrong thing very well. Doing the wrong things well gives you confidence in what you do, but may keep you from accomplishing what you need to do. Politicians who know how to do television and media advertising have had to learn (often by sad experience) that the Internet changes the rules of the game and requires doing something new.

- Don't just focus on small improvements that seemingly avoid risk but that fail to appropriately redefine your customers, products, or industry when they are changing around you. At times strategy requires bold, innovative thinking where you try to anticipate customer problems before customers are even aware of them. Few customers requested through market research to have a satellite mapping system where they could map

their home and directions to other locations.
Google innovators anticipated an unmet
opportunity with Google Earth and the products
that subsequently flowed from it.

• Be wary of strategic pandering in which you make
different promises to various stakeholders. You
cannot ride two horses with one behind. Being all
things to all people generally results in succeeding
with none.

Recognizing and trying to avoid these pitfalls is not
enough. If you are going to be a strategist, your fundamental rule is to be clear about where you are going. Gaining
this clarity comes when you master four strategy principles.
Principles turn assumptions and beliefs into convictions and
commitments. Mastering these four strategy principles will
help you be clear about where you are going.

STAY CURIOUS TO DEVELOP
A POINT OF VIEW ABOUT YOUR
OWN FUTURE

As head of R&D for Nike, it would be easy for John Hoke
to focus on the latest fads in shoe and clothing fashion.
Instead, he tries to anticipate in multiple dimensions
the future in which Nike will work, and develop Nike

products that no one else will be able to beat. Part social anthropologist, part designer, part technologist, all student, he learns everything he can about the psyche of the next generation, the future of cutting-edge design, and the possibilities that weird science will bring.

As a strategist, Hoke is able to assimilate these three seemingly independent areas to create breakthrough possibilities. In a particularly interesting example that also serves as a metaphor for his approach, Hoke's endless quest for practical new ideas led him to discover the company Z Corporation, a desktop manufacturer that uses hydrocarbons to "print" designs not on paper, but in three dimensions to create a physical object rather than a mere visual representation. Hoke immediately saw the possibilities for footwear: instead of a large and complex supply chain, the customer could have his or her foot scanned into a prototype, and the printer could then print a customized shoe. As a strategist, Hoke seeks to redefine the future.

In a different twist on strategic leadership, consider the case of Nokia, the world's largest mobile device manufacturer. Despite having coinvented the mobile phone industry over the past twenty years, Nokia executives realized that their strategy of manufacturing devices was limiting. They recognized that Nokia needed to also become an Internet company that produced content for its cellular devices to compete in the emerging Internet world.

Nokia's fiercest competitors would no longer come from the traditional telecommunications field but instead from virtually anywhere that smart software designers could dial in. Nokia needed to be smarter, quicker, more flexible, more in tune with the latest in technology and the consumer.

CEO Ollie-Pekka Kallasvuo called on the entire Nokia organization to reexamine every role, every process, every structure and system, every relationship, and every assumption: partners, investments, products, and geography. The focus was to become an Internet company, not just a company focused on manufacturing devices. It is because of strategic actions such as this that Nokia is considered to be one of the top companies for leadership in the world.

What can you do to stay curious about the future and develop your unique point of view? You need to have a sense of possibility and access new ideas that may take you out of your comfort zone.

- *Always ask yourself: "What if . . ." and explore possibilities*: When you read a novel, go to a movie, go to a restaurant, or go shopping, be looking at what you might learn from each of these experiences about your product or services. For example, we better understood about referral hiring (asking an employee to refer a friend, which better commits the employee who made the referral) by noticing that we did not change lines in grocery stores when someone got in line behind us—that line behavior in grocery stores might have an impact on hiring practices.

- *Connect with leading thinkers who may be customers, investors, employees, or competitors*: We don't generally learn innovative ideas from those with whom we have strong ties (close friendships) because we often choose friends who share many of our ideas. We need to have many weak ties (more casual contacts) with people not like us who may give us insights we may not otherwise have. Find and nurture these diverse relationships so that you can see new ways to see your world.

- *Read broadly*: One CEO of a *Fortune* 500 company tells people that he secretly likes to read *Rolling Stone* and *People* magazines even though he knows most of his peers read only business books and trade journals.

- *Make technology your friend if it is not one already*: Technology will profoundly affect every business going into the future. Become a serious student of the future by reading books and searching Web sites that talk about global trends in economics, demographics, and politics; and reflect on their impact for your industry, organization, and people. At times it is interesting to simply to do a Google search on a problem or challenge you might be facing. See what others have done and how they have approached the problem. Use the Internet to access not only information but to forge relationships you might not otherwise have.

- *Learn to experience problems that your best future customers might be facing*: Act like a customer of your company's products or services. See yourself through their eyes. Don't just ask them what they want, but experience firsthand what they experience.

By doing the above you will be more willing to shift and broaden the organization's image of itself. Ketchum, a division of Omnicom and one of the world's largest and most successful public relations firms, engaged 250 of its top leaders in a strategic reassessment of the firm's identity in the virtual, viral Internet world. As a result, it has recast both its self-definition and its offer from that of "a public relations firm" to a "communications agency" to better accommodate new ways of reaching people that are outside the traditional PR box.

In another sort of exercise, instead of only looking at organizations inside their own industries, great strategists can look at and learn about ways that firms in analogous industries have distinguished themselves in their industry to attain superior results. For example, members of the hotel industry could look at airlines, food services, and theme parks as sister consumer service businesses and pick up some very useful ideas about what can happen and how to capitalize on those possibilities.

INVITE YOUR SAVVIEST OUTSIDERS INSIDE

What's the acid test for your strategy? That it positions your company to compete over the long run. Competitiveness means that you do something unique that your customers value. When this happens, your investors have increased confidence in your future and your employees see the connection between their daily actions and long-term customer expectations. It also means engaging with other players who could affect the future of firm—important community member and other activists.

How does customer involvement affect strategy? Isn't "customer focus" really a role for marketing or sales?

Customer involvement influences strategy when their needs and experiences connect to what each person in the organization can and should do to serve those customers. The ingenious technology chip that allowed an appliance (washing machine, dryer, or refrigerator) to self-diagnose and contact a repairperson to come to the house to fix it sounded brilliant in the boardroom but failed to launch an ease-of-ownership business strategy for the simple reason that most homeowners prefer some warning before random repairpersons show up in their homes.

Beau Parnell, who now runs leadership development at Microsoft, tells the story of how Cisco became more connected to customers when he was there. He recounted that John Chambers, Cisco's CEO, asked Parnell to take on a strategic corporate initiative to create a customer engineering "certification" program and process. Cisco's equipment was not user-friendly, and the industry had very little in the way of actual troubleshooting frameworks. Parnell began by pulling together key thinkers from around the company to become the Top Gun team (as the project was called). Since this program was being built for the engineers in Cisco's customers, Parnell and his colleagues believed that Top Gun would be incomplete without involving a really tough customer. Although most of the company thought Parnell had lost his mind, he invited Cisco's toughest external critic to join the team.

We'll call him "Joe." Whenever Joe was anywhere near Cisco headquarters, the team joked that alarm bells would sound, since Joe was one of the leading thinkers in networks and troubleshooting, and he frightened even Cisco's best engineers.

Here's how Parnell tells the story: "Joe agreed to join our team and was with us on every move. He previewed certification-training manuals and tested out troubleshooting scenarios. His stamp of approval was on every document or process. Seven months later the Top Gun team delivered the CCIE (Certified Cisco Internetworking Engineer) process worldwide. It had a very tough critic's recommendation and credibility. The CCIE has since become a worldwide standard, and those holding the credential command serious hiring bonuses." When the process was complete, Joe confided that he had been preparing a recommendation that his company drop Cisco as their supplier just as Cisco was inviting him to join the team. Instead, he became a raving fan.

John Chambers was so pleased with this effort that he bought each of the team members a leather Navy pilot's jacket with team names embroidered on it. The company bought one for Joe, but because of the rules against giving gifts to customers, it was placed in a glass case on the wall in headquarters. Two years later, when Joe in fact decided to join Cisco, the company had a glass-breaking ceremony.

Customers identify with and value the products and services of your firm. Without their enthusiastic acceptance of the products and services that will be newly made available through any new strategy, the strategy would have been better left as a term paper. These lead customers are the thought leaders that others follow. This consideration in large part drove Nokia's decision to change: it needed the users of Web 3.0, especially the N–Gen (next-generation users), to identify with Nokia as a cool, savvy, cutting-edge partner for content creation on the Internet, not as an engineering-driven device company. No accident that Nokia's corporate slogan evolved to, simply, "Connecting people."

Strategic leaders find out why customers initially choose their product and why customers quit using their product. Consider how Unilever created mock kitchens so it could watch customers use its products, then decided instead to go directly into customers' homes to remove as much artificiality as possible in the observed experience with Unilever products. Bill Marriott claims to read all the feedback forms filled out by customers to find out what they want more of or less of from Marriott hotels. He then brings the customers' perspectives into decision making by sharing this information throughout the organization. Marriott seeks employee insights on customers as well. The hotel chain understands its customers so well that even if customers are not physically present, their ideas and interests are.

Strategically customer-focused leaders are passionate consumers of their own products so that they can experience the customer experience firsthand. David Motyl, formerly CEO of Amtico International flooring, had Amtico floor products installed throughout each home that he and his family lived in over a twenty-year period— a total of six houses and apartments—so that he could understand any issues of installation, maintenance, and wear from the customer's point of view.

To bring discipline to understanding customers, we have devised a simple exercise. First, we ask managers to identify their top customers. Most can identify the leading customers, those who are industry leaders, who purchase a lot of the products or services you sell, and who buy from you. We then ask managers to predict why these customers buy from them. We often have managers divide one hundred points among common customer buying criteria: products/services, customer relationships, technology, distribution or access, price, or other criteria. Then we ask customers the same question to find out if managers inside the company have the same buying criteria as customers outside the company. Finally, we ask managers to find ways to build increased connection with the targeted customers by including the customers in product discussions (à la Cisco), management actions (Nokia regularly invites customers to management training activities), or shaping company culture. By identifying key customers, learning their buying criteria, and involving them in building an organization to serve them, companies are able to move beyond servicing to anticipating and partnering with key customers (see figure 2-1 for the worksheet to do this exercise).

In addition to customers, strategists also respond to other external stakeholders. The larger the company, the greater impact it has on the world. Investors and the larger community will have a stake in and reaction to your strategy. The financial community and capital markets have to believe in the strategy if they are to support it through the market price of stocks and other corporate paper. Such support shows up in intangibles that ensure confidence in the future such as meeting quarterly earnings targets, having strategic clarity, supporting core

FIGURE 2-1

Increase share of customer

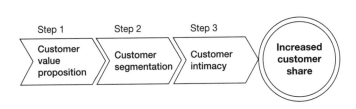

technical competencies, and building enabling organization capabilities.

The community is another critical stakeholder that strategists must consider. We have discovered that corporate social responsibility is rooted in living a set of accepted values. If your strategy requires child labor in Indonesia, ripping the top off a mountain in a mineral-rich developing nation, firing two-thirds of the workforce in a small town in the United States dependent on one factory for its economic life, or driving employees to make unethical decisions to meet unreasonable goals, think again. But beyond living values, corporate social responsibility has to do with sustainability and finding a way to consume fewer resources. Wal-Mart has asked its toy suppliers to reduce packaging; it has worked hard to have more energy-efficient buildings that have a smaller carbon footprint. At any one point in time 35 percent of IBM's workforce is not in an office, but mobile, which saves office space and driving time to and from work. Social responsibility also deals with philanthropy as organizations give back to the world in which they operate through financial donations, but also through encouraging employees to donate time to good causes. In a world filled with activists enabled by viral communications, everything a company does can be expected to be known instantly. Firms like Mitsubishi and DuPont have installed chief sustainability officers who monitor how well the firms work in their environments.

ENGAGE THE ORGANIZATION—NO "ONE" KNOWS ENOUGH

Rather than work by yourself or with a small exclusive group of trusted advisers—or even customers—you need to engage others within the organization in developing your strategy. Why? Because each member of the organization has a point of view worth hearing about how the strategy will be operationalized internally, and should have a point of view about how that strategy will affect the customer. The research on self-employed individuals is counterintuitive. Self-employed people work longer hours, but enjoy their jobs much more. Why? Because they have a line of sight about how their work impacts the business. The more people are involved in strategy discussions, the more likely they will be to be engaged in defining and delivering the strategy.

At Wal-Mart, for example, a gracious administrative assistant who made sure our visit was well coordinated hosted us. When we asked her how she liked working at Wal-Mart, she said it was the best job she could imagine. When we asked why, she told us that she made a difference in this company that would soon reach $500 billion in revenue. She felt once that the bread Wal-Mart sold was not meeting the standards that she, a consumer, felt it should meet. So, she met with the person in charge of supplying bread for Wal-Mart. He listened to her ideas and invited her to share them with the bread supplier, who also listened. The bread sold by Wal-Mart was different because of her ideas. She also said she had other ideas she would soon share and that Wal-Mart encouraged such employee participation in the products and services it offers.

Nokia has worked to make the process of shaping strategy as open and transparent as possible. Its leaders, with help from its change staff, have held large town meetings, called *cafés*, in all the regions in which they operate around the world during their strategic development process. Another creative approach is to establish an internal advocacy process where industry data is shared openly, and participants in the strategic process—often senior executives—are divided into groups where they must advocate a particular direction of growth for the business. In these groups, the leaders are not looking for the "correct" answer; they are charged with advocating a strategic position. Once each group has formulated a compelling strategy for itself along with implications from the same data set, they come together to decide which strategic option is best.

TABLE 2-1

Strategy process calendar

Month	Activities
January	Meeting for top 2–3% of company leaders where the annual "theme" is laid out in a three-day meeting
	One day spent by each business unit (product, geography, or function) discussing how the corporate agenda for the year affects it
February	Management bonus criteria set according to key theme
March	People nominated for corporate development based on the theme for the year
April–May	Major strategy reviews to review each division's plans for the year: business challenges laid out with financial, talent, and technology requirements
June	Rating of each employee on how well they performed
	Stock options allocated based on the performance
July	Strategy business planning for the next year
August	Presentation to the board of last year's plan, this year's plan, and first discussion of next year's theme
September–October	Creation of operating plans: updating targets, implementing corporate initiatives, reviewing talent and financial requirements
November	Follow-up on plans for the last year; debrief on what worked and what did not
December	Preparation for the next year

Employees also find it helpful to have a clear and consistent governance process for how strategy is deployed. One company has a regular and predictable strategy process calendar so that employees can anticipate the flow of strategy through the company and so that they can connect the pieces of strategy (see table 2-1).

In this company, employees know what to expect about planning. When employees can actively participate in deciding where you are going, they will help you make a better decision about where you are going and help make sure that you get there.

CREATE STRATEGIC TRACTION
WITHIN THE ORGANIZATION

Strategic leadership also requires embedding strategic capability throughout the organization. Strategy thinking is often delegated upward to the CEO or senior management team, who have a legitimate responsibility to shape the direction of the entire company. But strategic traction comes when employees at all levels of the company not only understand where the company is going, but are excited by it, remember it, and know what to do to make it happen in their day-to-day decisions.

As we have looked at hundreds of vision, mission, purpose, strategy, or goal statements, we have identified six criteria that we call the *ABC's of strategic traction* for any organization (see figure 2-2). These criteria enable leaders at any level to be clear about where they want to go.

Aspirational. For the strategy to take hold, employees need to believe in the values inherent in it: they need an emotional connection at a very personal level. Former U.S. president John F. Kennedy's simple, emotional speech in 1963 launched a renewed space program: "I believe that this nation should commit itself to achieving the goal, before this decade is out, of landing a man on the moon and returning him safely to the earth." Kennedy's strategy was a clear appeal to a nation's best sense of self, with

FIGURE 2-2

ABCs of strategic traction

Aspirational	Strategy focuses on the future and is seen as something challenging that employees can aspire to achieve.
Behaviors	Strategy translates vision into concrete actions and behaviors.
Customer orientation	Strategy delineates how to meet and exceed customer expectations.
Discipline	Strategy shows up in organizational capabilities and management processes (staffing, training, budgeting, information technology).
Energize	Strategy creates an emotional connection with employees' own personal needs and desires.
Focus	Strategy concentrates organizational resources and employee attention on a few key priorities.

stunning results. Imagine the commitment that grew in every NASA employee at those words.

Behaviors. Values-based intentions must translate into concrete actions and behaviors if they are to be credible. One approach to identifying those behaviors: vet a draft values statement with employees and ask three questions:

- Do the internal values we propose as a corporation matter to you? If not, what values would be?

- What actions would make these values real to you? What would we do more of? Less of? Stop? Start?

- If the firm lives these values, are you more likely to help make the strategy succeed?

Customer Orientation. Strategic leaders need to translate external customer expectations into the organization's culture. In other words, customer expectations need to drive the behaviors of leaders and employees, from the systems used to hire, train, and pay employees to the messages the leadership shares. To start, strategic leaders need to ask themselves: Am I as a leader behaving in a way that connects customer expectations to employee actions? Is my organization the employer of choice for the employees that my customers would choose? If a customer saw our performance management system, would they be pleased with the behaviors and outcomes specified? Would a customer be delighted with the training and communication being offered? When internal management practices align with customer expectations, the culture supports the customer expectations.

Corporate values can also matter to the customer. A firm's values are part of its offer to the marketplace. The rise of Whole Foods and other "green" organizations is recent proof of this phenomenon. Even companies with scant historical interest in such things are shifting strategies to reflect the change in consumer values. Wal-Mart, relentlessly focused for its entire existence on low cost, is suddenly the world's largest seller of energy-efficient LED bulbs and organic milk. Customers want their own aspirations realized, and want their purchases to help. Ask them:

- Are the internal values we propose of value to you as our customer? If not, what values would be?

- What would make these espoused values real to you? This question generates dialogue that can be quite wonderful and revealing about the behaviors that would enable the firm to treat customers better.

- Finally, if we live these values and behave as you suggest, will you increase our share of your business?

Discipline. Since the business world has dedicated the last two decades to downsizing, rightsizing, de-layering, outplacing, and reengineering, it may come as a surprise to learn that organizations are not really about their management levels. Think about it: do any customers know or care about the number of management levels in your company? No. But they do know what it does well. An organization's identity comes from its ability to do something well (like meeting the needs of the users of Web 3.0) because it has some special organizational talents: an ability to collaborate, learn, change with speed, change culture, innovate, serve customers, be efficient, be accountable, etc. Strategists must constantly be shaping both the strategy and organization at the same time, starting at the outside and working toward the inside.

The bottom line: the job of strategic formulation is not done until the organization clearly knows how to engage around it, including those employees below the level of SVP. Organizational disciplines aligned to the strategy can make a significant difference: financial disciplines to strategically allocate budget; technology disciplines to manage the flow of information; marketing and sales disciplines to translate customer desires into products or services; engineering disciplines to design products; manufacturing disciplines to produce on time and on budget; and human resource disciplines to manage talent and organization.

Sometimes this work of strategic clarification requires leaders to more fundamentally rethink and redefine their organizations, as Ollie-Pekka Kallasvuo and other leaders did throughout Nokia. Often, it is simply a discipline of making sure that the company is organized in every detail to meet customer needs.

Energize. Employees need a second kind of emotional connection: one that ties into their hopes for their own futures (a "What's in it for me and my family?" connection). Metrics will only go so far in creating the necessary customer-focused behaviors needed to enact the strategy. A compelling strategy that engages people in creating their own futures energizes them. Kellogg enlists its people not just in selling cereal and snack food but also helping the world to eat healthier foods. In fact, Kellogg's snack food is internally referred to as "wholesome snacks."

Focus. Strategy is as much about saying no as it is about saying yes. Being willing to stay on task and not divert time, attention, and other resources to nonstrategic temptations will make the strategy succeed.

CONCLUSION: STRATEGY AS STORY

A strategy created with these four principles added together becomes a story, a story with a goal, customers, employees, means, ends, and outcomes. A good story appeals to the mind (clever, insightful), the heart (emotive), and the feet (leads to action). Leaders as strategists can tell the story about their organization to employees inside and investors and customers outside. It also becomes part of the leader's personal story as she constantly stays on message about the goals and how to make them happen. Challenge yourself to see whether your organization has a coherent story (see assessment 2-1).

WHAT DOES THIS STRATEGY DISCUSSION add up to? Rightsize your strategy based on the best information available, then engage customers, employees, and anyone else who matters to the process. Keep the community and investors in mind. Think large, but also realize that overly grandiose visions strain credulity: the "sweet spot" is to rightsize the strategy so that it stretches but does not snap the organization. Good strategists take a realistic perspective about their technical and social capabilities and build on them. Building capabilities to best in class takes years, so any strategy that ignores what the company does well does so at its peril.

So how do you know if you are a good strategist? Answer the question about where you are going by assessing whether you have a point of view about the future of your organization and industry. Have you really been curious about where you could go, or have you been

ASSESSMENT 2-1

Strategy quick challenge

Can your organization tell a consistent strategy story?

Quick challenge: Select five to seven individuals in your organization (in different functional areas) and ask them to answer the questions below that pertain to your organization's strategy. Determine how close the answers are.

1. What is our organization's strategy?

   Who are our target customers, and why do they buy from us?

   _____

   _____

   _____

2. Who are our largest competitors, and how do they try to differentiate themselves from us?

   _____

   _____

   _____

3. How do our profits compare against those of our top competitors?

   _____

   _____

   _____

4. What top two to four industry trends will most affect our organization?

   _____

   _____

   _____

5. What do you see as the company's most important tasks/priorities over the next twelve to twenty-four months?

   _____

   _____

   _____

   _____

going through the motions? Are your customers excited to go into that future with you? Your employees? Other stakeholders?

Go to www.leadershipcodebook.com for a video of Norm Smallwood explaining the customer value proposition and the strategic options matrix. On that site you will also find another premium leadership code tool on strategy.

THREE

Rule 2

Make Things Happen

To make things happen, be an *executor*:

1. Make change happen.

2. Follow a decision protocol.

3. Ensure accountability.

4. Build teams.

5. Ensure technical proficiency.

EXECUTION IS MAKING SURE that you get where you are going. Knowing where you are going and getting there are two very different challenges. We often know where we want to go and what we should do, but we don't do it well. At a personal level, we know we should exercise, eat healthily, and spend time with those we love, but in the inevitable rush of life, too often we don't do these things as well as we would like. Execution is the ability to turn what we know into what we do.

As a leader, your ability to execute will enable you to turn strategic aspirations into actions, desires into results, and desired futures into present reality. By being able to execute, you enable others to see how a future vision will affect their actions today. The ability to execute is also highly practical. Short-term success can be the engine that will drive the organization forward and reach the tipping point that makes strategy happen. Ability to execute instills disciplines that enable you to produce the right skills, further institutional knowledge, and—let's be real—make money. The better you execute, the more money you will have to meet current obligations, to fund future investment, and to create a safety net in case of difficulties or to capitalize on opportunities yet unforeseen. Execution without strategy may be blind, but strategy without execution is unfounded hope.

Over the last several years, Procter & Gamble (P&G) has undergone a fundamental transformation. Under the watch of CEO A. G. Lafley, P&G has set its sights on a new strategy and then has been an execution machine in the midst of large-scale change. Others may have good ideas, but P&G has been able to have them and execute them in a manner that has catapulted its results to the top of the industries in which it competes—all this and acquire and merge Gillette into its distinctive culture as well. Perhaps one of P&G's secret weapons is that employees tend to stay for their whole career and so over time they get to know each other, and this helps them get things done.

In our work and study, we have found execution constants. Leaders who execute connect the present to the future, focus on linking the short term to the long term, manage their time, engage others, and ensure accountability and consequences for delivering on time. These leaders accept responsibility for what needs to happen, do what needs to be done, and develop a convincing track record of delivering results. They keep promises to multiple stakeholders. In short, they follow the five fundamental execution disciplines we share below.

MAKE CHANGE HAPPEN

Execution inevitably requires making change happen. No system or process is ever in stasis these days: customer needs evolve, technologies improve, continuous innovations are required, and new opportunities arise just as existing opportunities dry up. The changes may be incremental and relatively small—a tightening of the nuts and bolts in a process that generally works pretty well. Or it may be larger systemic changes brought about by a new strategic course, as we have already discussed with Nokia and P&G. In either case, excellence in execution inevitably requires leaders to play a role in making change happen. A CEO told us that a company that took fifty years to build might be lost in fewer than two years if it could not respond to change.

As a change agent, you need to be aware of both making individual change events happen and changing underlying patterns or cultures. Changing events means building disciplines to accomplish projects on time and within budget. Some of these projects might be relatively minor (a launch of a new product) or major (integrating a merger or acquisition or implementing a new information system). We have learned that making projects happen comes when you bring a set of change disciplines to a project. From work with leading companies, we have identified questions you should make sure are raised and answered around any change project (see assessment 3-1).

- *To what extent are strong leaders assigned to this project?*
  Leadership support for a change initiative means
  that you assign top talent to key initiatives. Employees can sense commitment to a project by who is
  assigned to lead it. Then, these assigned leaders
  need to pass a calendar test (do they spend 20 to 30
  percent of their time on this project?), a passion test

(do they show energy and enthusiasm for the project?), and a public accountability test (are they willing to be a spokesperson for the project?).

- *To what extent is there a clear need for the project?* The leaders need to build a case for change, to help people see that the reasons for the project are greater than the resistance to the project. Sometimes short-term failures (e.g., losing money, customers, or market opportunities) create a clear rationale for change and you simply need to capitalize on these realities. At other times, you need to create an image of what can be if you were to change.

- *To what extent do we have a clear direction for the change?* As a leader, you need to define success in measurable, trackable, and clear terms. A CEO dedicated to innovation went public with the goal of having 50 percent of revenues from products created in the last two years. This clarity helped people rally behind the changes required to make this happen. Leaders throughout the organization can set similar public goals commensurate with the size and level of the change effort.

- *Do we have buy-in and commitment from the people necessary to implement the change?* People commit when they have information about why the change needs to occur and how they can tie a change to their daily behaviors. One of the reasons P&G has been so successful is that over a long period of time, most employees have come to believe that the company can be trusted to do the right thing. This is a tremendous advantage over companies whose employees are concerned that the company may have ulterior motives for changes. Any leader's job is to share information so that people know why the change needs to occur and to help people define the personal day-to-day impact of the change on their work. A senior leader in one company, in addition to doing a video, blog, and other communications about change, asked each leader to have discussions about the changes and their implications for local work groups. When leaders throughout the company went public with their commitment, they became more committed.

- *To what extent do we break up the change into decisions that need to be made in the near term?* Large-scale changes need to be broken into smaller chunks that are doable in short time frames (generally ninety days). We have also found that when the decisions that the change requires are clearly defined, they are likely to be made and change happens. Some companies build large action plans when they might be better off with rigorous decision protocols.

- *To what extent are we able to institutionalize the change?* Change leaders shift the focus of a change from their personal agenda to organizational processes. Changes become institutionalized when they show up in how resources are allocated through a budgeting process, how people are treated (hired, developed, and paid), and how information systems gather and share data. You need to make sure that the support functions align their practices to sustain the changes you envision.

- *To what extent do we measure and learn from the change efforts?* Rarely do changes occur exactly as you plan. Learning by observing, measuring, and adapting is a key leadership role. Learning requires periodic checkups and monitoring to figure out what is working and what is not working to bring about change.

These questions may be familiar, but need to be asked rigorously to develop a change discipline in your organization. If you regularly apply these questions to your

ASSESSMENT 3-1

Change checklist

To turn what we know about change into what we do to make change happen, we have identified seven key factors of successful change. Think of these as a pilot's checklist for change. You can determine the likelihood of any change project's success by asking these seven questions. The profile that results will help you know how likely the change will be to succeed and highlight where your need to focus to improve.

Scale: 1 = Low ◄ - - ► 10 = High

Leadership support: To what extent does this project have adequate leadership support?   1 2 3 4 5 6 7 8 9 10

Clear need: To what extent is there a clearly shared understanding of the need for the project?   1 2 3 4 5 6 7 8 9 10

Clear outcome: To what extent does this project have a clear outcome?   1 2 3 4 5 6 7 8 9 10

Stakeholder buy-in: To what extent do we have buy-in and commitment from the people necessary to implement the project?   1 2 3 4 5 6 7 8 9 10

Decision process: To what extent do we know the decisions   1 2 3 4 5 6 7 8 9 10 that need to be made in the next ninety days to make progress on the project?

Dedicated resources: To what extent have the changes inherent in the project been institutionalized by dedicating key resources of information, money, and talent?   1 2 3 4 5 6 7 8 9 10

Monitoring and learning: To what extent do we have measures in place for ongoing learning and progress checks as the project proceeds?   1 2 3 4 5 6 7 8 9 10

Scoring:

Change initiatives must receive high marks in all areas to achieve success. Evaluate each area against this scale:
9–10 = Excellent | 7–8 = Good |
6 and below = Project may be at risk in this area

projects, you will be better able to execute what needs to be done. As the pace of change increases, leaders must learn to manage change rather than let it manage them, to help the organization and individuals grow more comfortable with the ambiguity inherent in any change, and to help others see change as an opportunity, not a problem. In leading change, leaders must have the discipline to turn what they know into what they do.

Being disciplined about these change questions helps leaders manage change much the way a pilot's checklist helps the pilot fly a plane, a surgeon's checklist for surgery increases successful outcomes, or a fast-food restaurant has a clear checklist for employees to follow. Leading change with a disciplined checklist turns what we know about change into what we do.

Sustainability . . . Make Change Last. Change can often be an event; we do something once, but it is not a pattern that endures over time. Leaders who use the change checklist in assessment 3-1 can often create faster and more disciplined events. They can make things happen. But when the leader leaves, there is quick relapse to "what was."

Transforming change from events that can be coerced into sustainable patterns often requires looking for fundamental causes as to why the change does not occur. Over the last twenty years, we have kept track of what we call *change viruses*, or reasons why changes do not last over time (see figure 3-1 for a list of some of the most common of these viruses). Each item on our list has a story behind it and has happened in at least half a dozen organizations.

To create new patterns requires that these viruses be identified and discussed. Any of us in a relationship for a long period of time learn that there are often "unspeakables" or things we don't want, or don't know how, to talk about. The longer we don't speak about the unspeakables, the more harm they do to the relationship. When we can find a way to speak about these issues and discuss them with some degree of detachment, we can often resolve them and make progress.

In organizations, we call these unspeakable patterns viruses because they infect the organization. And there are patterns that happen without us being fully aware of them. Through complacency or inertia, we overlook some of these patterns. When we visit the houses of family or friends, we are often quick to see the dirt or clutter that they no longer see (and vice versa). But, like a virus (physical or computer), once we label the virus—talk about it—we can generally become immune to it.

Execution requires not only that change occur, but that new patterns emerge as old patterns are exposed and expunged. The virus detection and elimination exercise offers a way for you to build sustainable execution.

FIGURE 3-1

Common viruses preventing change

Sometimes organizations develop patterns that keep change from happening. We call these patterns viruses *because they can be diagnosed as organizational illnesses that can generally be cured. The following are a sampling of some of the most common viruses we have identified. By asking each member of your management team to pick the top two or three, you can make explicit what your viruses are within your organization. Once they are identified, you can begin to resolve them.*

1. Overinform

   We tell everyone even before we have a meeting. We make sure everyone has been informed, then have a meeting that only slows things down.

2. Have it my way

   We don't learn from each other: we suffer from not-invented-here syndrome.

3. Saturday morning quarterback

   We criticize things, even before they happen.

4. False positive

   We do "nice-talk" (especially in public); we are overly kind even if we disagree. This leads to false positive.

5. Concealed consensus

   We confuse participation with consensus. We think that everyone has to agree before we act, so people say they agree when they don't.

6. Forward to our past: Look in the rearview mirror

   We are so afraid of losing our heritage that we don't change our culture; we are locked into our habits.

7. Caste: value by grade

   We judge people by their title and rank rather than performance or competence.

8. Turfism: My business versus "our" business

   We defend our turf, sometimes to the detriment of the overall organization.

9. Command and control

   We like to make sure that senior managers run the company and delegate responsibility up; this keeps us from feeling a personal obligation to change.

10. Hard on the people instead of the problem

    We attack a colleague personally, rather then attacking the problem.

*For a complete list of change viruses and a short video explaining how to
use the virus list with your team, please visit our Web site*
www.leadershipcodebook.com

FOLLOW A DECISION PROTOCOL

Decision making is at the core of intelligent action. How
the leader thinks about, makes, and carries out decisions
signals the leader's persona. A pattern of decisions shapes
an identity, not only for the leader herself, but for
"who we are" as a team, a division, or an enterprise, and
how we go about executing. A leader chooses how
much time to spend on any single issue, whom to spend
time with, what information to process, what meetings
to hold, and what issues come to her attention. Through
a pattern of decisions, a leader creates an identity and sets
an important example. Clear decisions launch focused and
timely actions while ambiguity delays actions, or forces
other people to guess the next thing to do—sometimes
wrongly. (Assessment 3-2 lays out a protocol that
can help you clarify your thinking on decisions, and
figure 3-2 provides a matrix you can use to structure your
decisions.)

One of the most effective execution-oriented leaders
we know approached most questions and problems from

ASSESSMENT 3-2

A protocol for decision making

Scale: 1 = Low ◄ - - ► 10 = High

Clarity

We are precise about the decisions we are making.　　1 2 3 4 5 6 7 8 9 10

When we have a decision to make, we focus on　　1 2 3 4 5 6 7 8 9 10
two to three options or alternatives.

We begin presentations by being clear about the decision　1 2 3 4 5 6 7 8 9 10
that must be made as a result of the discussion.

We break big ideas (customer service, globalization)　1 2 3 4 5 6 7 8 9 10
into specific decisions with clear alternatives.

Accountablility

We know who is responsible for a decision and hold　1 2 3 4 5 6 7 8 9 10
that person (or team) accountable.

Consensus does not mean equal vote. Someone　1 2 3 4 5 6 7 8 9 10
(or team) is responsible.

Timeliness

We have public deadlines for when decisions will　1 2 3 4 5 6 7 8 9 10
be made, and we stick to them.

We are demanding about getting decisions done—if　1 2 3 4 5 6 7 8 9 10
the team lags, the manager decides.

Process

We create ownership for the decision by engaging　1 2 3 4 5 6 7 8 9 10
the people who will implement it.

We take appropriate risks for the decision as required.　1 2 3 4 5 6 7 8 9 10

We make clear the process we will use to make a　1 2 3 4 5 6 7 8 9 10
high-quality decision.

Return and report

Once we have made a decision, we follow up to ensure　1 2 3 4 5 6 7 8 9 10
that it is implemented.

Total:_____

*Evaluate each section of the assessment to determine your group's
strengths and weaknesses in that area, then look at the total score to
determine your organization's decision-making ability.*

FIGURE 3-2

Organization decision making worksheet

Principles	Application	
	Meetings In our meetings, how can we apply these principles?	**Projects** For key projects how can we apply these principles?
Clarity What is the decision to be made? (What are the options for this decision?)		
Accountability Who will be accountable for the decision (individual or team)?		
Timeline When will the decision have to be made and announced?		
Process What information needs to be collected; who needs to be involved?		
Return and report How will we follow up to make sure that learning occurs after the results of the decision are clear?		

others with the opening question: "What decision do you want me to make coming out of this conversation?" This action-oriented question required the employees to own what they wanted and how they thought the leader could help. Another company began to manage day-to-day change better by simply requiring that the first (or second) slide of every PowerPoint presentation elucidate the decision that would result from the forthcoming presentation. This decision-oriented discipline moved meetings along and clarified expectations.

The following questions help create better discipline around decision making.

- *What is the decision that needs to be made?* Often,
  there are nearly limitless choices for any decision
  that needs to be made. Simple decisions can get
  complex very quickly. A decision to open or close
  a facility may become complex with choices
  around location, natural resources, human capital
  availability, regulatory and tax relief, closeness
  to customers, history and tradition, community
  support, and other political or social implications.
  To focus decision making, you should not look
  at endless possibilities, but at the top two or three
  options. A senior leader renowned for his ability
  to execute said that when people met with him,

he wanted them to have done their homework and homed in on the top two or three options that they felt most comfortable with. In a spirit of simplification, one company started to focus aggressively on the key choices, not all choices. Being clear about what the decision is that needs to be made and the options available simplifies and focuses attention.

- *Who is going to make the decision?* Leaders clarify decision rights. The busy leader must focus on the few key decisions he personally needs to make, or drown. Every decision he does not personally need to make gets delegated. Key change decisions may be about people (how to staff an initiative), money (how to fund an initiative), data (how to track an initiative), or accountability (how to follow up on an initiative). When literally dozens of items seem to require a leader's attention, ask: "What are the two or three decisions you can make, at your level, in the next thirty days?" The answer will likely be clear: If *I* am not going to make the decision, then who will? Will this decision be made by committee or by a person? Who is ultimately accountable for the decision? What will be the consequences? Decisions may be made in many ways: majority rule, team consensus, input from others, or by a key person alone. Determining decision rights and rules in advance or making decisions clarifies expectations around authority and accountability expectations. When people expect to have a vote and they only have a voice, they may feel left out. When people assume that nothing is done until there is a consensus, they may feel that their point of view was ignored if they did not get their way. Participation does not mean consensus. Being clear about who makes what decisions builds accountability—because if everyone is responsible, no one is accountable; but if one person is accountable, decisions will often be made.

- *When will the decision be made?* Almost all work will expand to fill the time provided. Deadlines generate commitment to action. As a leader, you can create public deadlines about when decisions will be made. In one company, once someone was assigned a decision (the above question), he was asked when he would present his recommendation or results. When the decision maker specified a specific time and place (e.g., "in staff meeting in six weeks"), the likelihood of decisions being made went up dramatically. Absent a deadline, dialogues become debates, and debates become endless.

- *How will we make a good decision?* Making a good decision starts by knowing the quality level the decision requires, as well as the level of acceptance required by others essential to its successful implementation. In terms of quality, does the decision require 99.9 percent accuracy before deciding (e.g., a matter of personal safety or security) or could a decision be made with 80 percent accuracy (e.g., a policy that could be adapted over time) but that really needs everyone to be on board before implementing? If quality is the key, the person accountable for the decision must have the knowledge and capability to meet the quality threshold. Making a good decision based primarily on quality requires involving key people in the process of making the decision. Then, the outcomes of the decision need to be monitored so that learning can occur.

As this decision protocol is followed, leaders pass the decisiveness and decision test. They not only know what they want, what the options are for getting there, which option works best, but they also have specified the key decisions that will only move the change along. They also shape a positive, decisive, execution-oriented identity for themselves and the organization.

ENSURE ACCOUNTABILITY

Accountability is at the heart of execution. Accountability means that an individual or team feels personal ownership and responsibility to get something done. Sometimes in large complex matrix organizations, so many people are responsible that no one is accountable. But even in smaller organizations, when there is no clear accountability about who will do what, execution languishes. Finger-pointing replaces action, and politics count more than results. Simply assigning accountability to someone is not enough. Accountability increases with standards, consequences, and feedback.

Standards. Accountability begins with clear and specific goals and measures. Ask a teenager to clean his room and, inevitably, he returns in moments "all done." We have not clearly and mutually defined the goal "clean." In fact, we have two vastly different standards. Standards allow us to answer the question: "How do we know if we have been successful?"

The huge literature on clear goal-setting highlights the characteristics of effective standards (what we call OPTIMAL goal setting):

*O*utcomes: They measure the result of what we will do.

*P*rocesses: They measure the processes by which we will do it.

*P*ublic: They are visible, and others know what they are.

*T*ime bound: They have deadlines for what is to be done.

*I*mportance-focused: They focus on the right things.

*M*anageable: They are within the control of the individual.

*A*ccepted: They are set with someone else, not imposed.

*L*earning: They use small failures as opportunities to learn how to improve rather than criticize and punish.

The best way to test standards is by asking your employees to repeat back to you their understanding of the goals and what they should be doing to achieve them. By listening carefully and correcting quickly, you can help clarify expectations. Your job is to make sure employees know what is expected of them so that they, not you, feel ownership for execution. When employees feel that your goals are their goals, your standards are their standards, and your desired outcomes their outcomes, you have successfully shared standards.

Consequences. Accountability also must have consequences for meeting or missing standards. A division manager went over budget in his first year, and received a letter from the corporate controller. The manager resolved to improve . . . until the other division managers let him in on the real consequences of going over budget: getting another form letter from accounting! How much accountability could he feel after that? Consequences count.

Consequences may be negative or positive. Negative consequences should let your employees know what they did wrong and how they can improve; positive consequences should be clear about what they did right and what they should continue to do. In either event, these conversations should be timely, behavior based, and candid. You set the tone for consequences in both public and private relationships. We have found that leaders sometimes have trouble holding direct reports accountable because of long-term relationships and history. When we asked executives what they would do differently in better executing a project, they inevitably said that they should have reacted more boldly and aggressively. When we push to identify what they should have done more boldly, the answer is almost always around people, and moving people who were not able to do the work required.

In addition to consulting technical experts in compensation, you should be the architect and owner of a reward system that aligns behavior and outcomes. A good reward system is performance based (when pay increases fail to reflect contribution, the system is meaningless as a consequence), transparent (people need to understand and respect why certain people get larger rewards), timely, durable, and widely distributed (overly top-heavy reward systems create an unhealthy, counterproductive class system).

Feedback. "Feedback," a sporting colleague of ours used to say, "Is the breakfast of champions. Inject Novocain into the legs of a champion skier and she will fail because she will get no feedback from the mountain." Only by completing the loop from outward action to inner understanding of the action's impact can anyone hope to understand his or her effect: what works, what doesn't, and what needs to improve. For you to be an effective executor, you need to both give and receive useful and timely feedback to the organization, to teams, and to individuals. You should be willing and able to receive feedback about yourself and model learning.

One of our clients consistently used a structured feedback methodology in her division. The five-step feedback process began with intentions ("What did we set out to do?"), then went to results ("What did we do?"), focused on the positive ("What did we do well?") before opening up discussion around mistakes ("What could we have done better?"), and concluded with learning ("What did we learn from this experience? What will we continue to do? What will we do better or differently?").

The results were remarkable. People quickly learned how to speak with each other more respectfully and with the goal of learning, not blaming. They also discovered a key operating habit of their organization—that team members rarely had a common understanding of what they were setting out to do. Armed with this collective insight, they were able to instill necessary disciplines around joint goal setting into their collective work process. They changed with remarkable speed, and the results were also remarkable. Interestingly, the change in atmosphere palpably improved from month to month. People were more open, more positive, and more engaged in their work. They knew how to work together.

Feedback is vital to the health and welfare of the organization and the people in it. Without a healthy approach to feedback, the basic human need to communicate can twist into gossip, backbiting, and misunderstanding. With an agreed-upon healthy way into conversations about working together for results, relationships and work processes will improve, and leaders will find that executing will be easier and more effective.

BUILD TEAMS

In large organizations, most execution work happens on teams because customer requirements as well as organizations are simply too complex for any one person to deliver against needs. Excellence in execution, then, depends on excellent teams. Teams bring together people with different skills and abilities to work toward a common goal, thereby inviting a variety of perspectives and encouraging new ideas, new approaches, and renewed commitment. Teams can also provide stability in times of flux in an organization: while individuals may trade in and out of a team because of shifting assignments and commitments, the team itself can continue as an independent identity with a sense a mission and, in effect, provide a productive holding environment for long-term initiatives. The team's collective commitment can progress the agenda.

Leaders executing through high-performing teams succeed at working four issues: setting a purpose backed by a process, managing roles/making decisions, building relationships, and learning. You can observe these four factors in teams you manage, and you can encourage leaders throughout your organization to do periodic team audits to make sure that teamwork exists in your organization.

Clear Purpose. Every team needs a clear charter for its existence ("Why are we here?") and ways of going forward ("What will we do and how?"). With high-performing teams, the purpose is both aspirational and energizing: it lays out an exciting set of stretch goals that are both professionally and personally rewarding, all structurally supported by deliverables and timelines. You can consistently track the extent to which the team is on or off target by asking if team members know why they are meeting.

Defined Governance Processes with Roles and Decision-Making Protocols. The governance issues surrounding roles and decision making need to be settled by the leader to ensure that each team member contributes optimally. Each individual needs to know what he or she contributes to the team ("Why am I here?") and in what way ("How will we work together?"). Decision making, then, concerns itself with the pace of progress (neither too fast nor too slow), with amount of information needed to make decisions (neither analysis paralysis nor lack of data), the right sort of participation (all members feel they can participate openly), and with the right amount of risk (not too high or too low).

Strong Relationships. Teams also work through seemingly paradoxical relationships. On the one hand, team members care about each other and show it by listening to each other, knowing each other personally, supporting each other in times of difficulty or crisis, and showing respect for ideas. We have all been on teams where, in times of crisis, we turn toward each other instead of away. These bonding and caring relationships sustain us in good times and bad. On the other hand, high-performing teams also manage differences and conflict by encouraging the sort of debate and dialogue that raise alternative points of view. Learning from your teammates how to improve is much better than learning from those who don't care about you.

Ongoing Learning. Finally, teams succeed through learning. Teams learn by periodically pausing, reflecting, and assessing. As a team, the members evaluate what has worked and what has not, looking for patterns and finding opportunities to improve. Leaders build team learning most powerfully by modeling learning behaviors: acknowledging personal successes and failures, staying curious and looking for new alternatives, and periodically conducting learning audits to review how the team has done.

ENSURE TECHNICAL PROFICIENCY

Leaders concerned about excellence in execution must be very concerned about technical proficiency in themselves and their organization. Being personally qualified in things that matter to those around you gives you credibility. Your technical proficiency may be financial, customer, operations, technology, or envisioning a future. Having a deep knowledge in an area enables you to lead not only by rhetoric but by reality. It allows you to ask probing questions in your area of expertise. As you move up through the organization, you may lose some of your current technical expertise, but having been excellent has positive legacy effects. You may not be the expert in all things, but it is good to be very gifted at some things.

In addition, you should ensure that your organization contains technical expertise. Do the people tasked with performing have the right skill sets? Are those skill sets even known? How can the organization be confident that the right people truly know their craft? What unique knowledge and skill does this set of problems require? Would we consider our knowledge as leading edge? If not, where is leading edge and how do we access it?

While ensuring technical proficiency may seem like a short-term goal—surely, skill sets will need to change—it has long-term consequences for the individual and the organization because most leaders begin careers by demonstrating technical excellence. Superior command of a technical skill set (e.g., in finance, operations, marketing, sales, engineering, law, etc.) grants a future leader great credibility and ensures the respect he will need to someday take up an important leadership position. The famous "halo effect" is true.

THE FUNDAMENTAL LEADERSHIP rule of execution is to make sure we get where we want to go. Execution is the ability to turn what we know into what we do. That ability depends on a variety of disciplines in change, decision making, accountability, teams, and technical excellence, as we have laid out. Some leaders are predisposed to execution and they naturally do the disciplines discussed; others can learn from the tools and diagnostic questions, and perform actions to become excellent as executors.

Go to www.leadershipcodebook.com for a video of Kate Sweetman illustrating how the viruses tool (figure 3-1) has worked at other companies to lower cultural barriers to execution success. On that Web site, you will also find a more complete and growing list of organizational viruses than you find on these pages, and to which you are invited to add your own. You will also find another premium leadership code tool on execution.

Rule 3

Engage Today's Talent

To engage today's talent, be a *talent manager*:

1. Communicate, communicate, communicate.

2. Create aligned direction; connect the individual to the organization.

3. Strengthen others; ensure people have the competencies they need.

4. Provide people with the resources to cope with demands.

5. Create a positive work environment—practice spiritual disciplines at work.

6. Have fun at work.

TALENT MANAGERS NURTURE and develop others. Leadership can never occur in isolation from followers. Leaders lead by engaging others in defining strategies and executing goals. Talent management has many parts. The easiest way to guarantee your company's success is to pick both your people and your competitor's people. We often joke that the most significant talent choice you could make is to place your lowest-performing employees in your competitor and hope they do for them what they did for you.

Managing talent is simple in principle, but not easy in practice. Successful talent managers get the most and the best out of their people. They are magnet managers for whom others like to work. They share credit for successes and take responsibility for failures. They are producers rather than consumers of talent for the rest of the company. They generate intense loyalty both to themselves as individuals and in the direction of the company. They have enough personal confidence to surround themselves with people who are gifted, and they make use of others' gifts. When people work for great talent managers they describe their experience in terms like: "I didn't know I could get so much done" and "There was a great sense of teamwork and connection with others." Talent managers are able to get things done in a way that is developmental and often inspiring. They also insist that people have fun.

No thoughtful leader today would deny the importance of talent. But, managing talent is more than slogans, token programs, and speeches. In our research we found that top companies for leadership have leaders who spend up to 30 percent of their time on talent issues. This time includes serious reviews of succession candidates, active participation in design and delivery of training and development programs, networking with high potentials, and discussion of talent at board and senior management meetings. You need to find ways to help people throughout your organization not only to feel intellectually engaged, but to have a sense of personal contribution to your organization's agenda. While hundreds of books have been written about upgrading talent, we have boiled it down to six talent resolutions that will improve the odds that the talent surrounding you performs at the highest level of which it is capable. Why *resolutions*, and not *principles* or *disciplines*? We like *resolution* because leading talent requires an act of will, even courage, to make it happen, much like a New Year's resolution.

COMMUNICATE, COMMUNICATE, COMMUNICATE

A leading company reworked its performance management system many times over ten years, always trying out the latest appraisal tools with no effect on performance. After a short study, we found that the real issue was that leaders in this firm were unable to have honest performance conversations with employees. They always hedged any negative feedback, regardless of the appraisal system. No new performance appraisal tool or system would ever fix this communication problem. If you are serious about retaining and developing talent you depend on, you need to connect with employees candidly through honest, open, and two-way dialogues.

In all of our research on communication, employees almost always claim to want more. This desire is legitimate: they are right in wanting to know why they are there, what is expected of them, and how they are doing toward that set of goals. To improve your ability to communicate, you need to remind yourself to be clear about what you want to say (the content), why you are saying it (supporting data, or the real nature of the problem, challenge, or opportunity), to whom you should say it (recognizing that there may be multiple audiences), how you should say it (communication methods), and when to share it (timing). If the effort is to engage others at their highest level of commitment, it is best to focus on only a few priorities and explain why those priorities are important. Too many priorities, and no one knows what to do. No rationale, and they find themselves wondering why any of this is important.

Communicate the reasons why, however, and these good people will gear themselves for action. When people know the *why*, they more readily accept the *what*.

As you communicate, you need to consider your audience, tailoring your message differently for the boardroom and the lunchroom, and learn to succeed in both. In addition, sharing information is not enough. People act on what they hear that appeals to their head and heart, and that accesses their hands and feet. You need to share your emotions and self, not just your intellectual ideas.

Master communicators personalize messages by sharing personal illustrations that others can relate to. Ray Wierzbicki, when head of professional services at Verizon, repeatedly made it clear that he wanted his people "skipping to work." He conveyed exactly what he meant by often sharing the story of his dad, a Polish immigrant who worked seven days a week in the small grocery he owned in New Jersey. According to Ray, his father never had a bad day at work because he had such a positive attitude that he skipped to work. That, of course, doesn't mean that the leader deals only in good news. Ray was always willing to lay out the challenges before his people completely. But master communicators share both bad and good news openly and directly, accepting blame for the bad and sharing credit for the good. In telling their stories, they create context, build on history, and create a future.

Finally, you need to keep constancy of message until it has been heard (more than until you are sick of saying it). Expect to share a message ten times for every one time that it will be heard and understood. These communication resolutions are not new, but if you do them, you will find that what you say matters more because people hear and act on it.

CREATE ALIGNED DIRECTION: CONNECT THE INDIVIDUAL TO THE ORGANIZATION

People in organizations need to work together collectively toward a common goal, and at the same time, they need to be able to express who they are individually. They need to approach the market and customers as one voice, and yet they need to be able to speak up as individuals. People need to work in an aligned direction, and they need to connect to the organization's purpose in a very personal way. Making these seeming paradoxes work is a key skill in managing talent.

A senior leader once told us that when he brought people onto his team, he would tell them: "If you and I think alike, one of us is not necessary. And it won't be me. But once we make a decision, we go forward with one voice." The talent manager finds gifted people with different skills capable of moving in the same strategic direction. To do so, he or she needs to create a shared purpose that helps each individual reach separate goals. At Herman Miller, R&D people want to improve on the science of office furniture; marketing and sales personnel want to identify and meet customer needs; manufacturing wants to create efficient and Six Sigma processes; and finance wants to ensure economic returns. CEO Brian Walker encourages each group to excel in their domain but connects everyone with the shared direction of "creating great places to live, work, and heal."[1] Each person understands how his role and the role of others contribute to the desired outcomes.

A simple, powerful exercise to help people align around strategy and assess their progress toward it is to have every member of your team identify his or her goals for the upcoming sixty or ninety days. Team members then post their lists publicly, and any team members can comment on each other's goals—what they would like to see more of and see less of. The peer feedback is then discussed, and adjustments made. As a result of this exercise, individual members deepen their understanding of how they can personally contribute to the strategy, and to the team overall. This public discussion of personal goals allows for individuality, but creates a shared sense of purpose and community. It also helps individuals be beholden to each other to reach their goals.

When individuals with different skills coalesce around a shared organizational purpose, another talent improvement practice takes place at a deeper level, connecting not just their short-term goals to the strategy but their sense of professional identity to the enterprise. When have done research on people's *career bests* (a specific period in their career when they felt they were performing at their own peak), we found four universal themes:

- Working together for a common good energizes almost everyone.

- People love to feel expert in their craft, whatever it may be.

- The more important the need, the greater the passion to fulfill it ("Making a difference" can be an organization philosophy).

- Career bests are all too rare—most people describe them as wistful memories.

Your job as talent manager is to help people connect their personal career best to the goals of the organization. An employee whose professional identity is rooted in design and innovation has a career best experience when her creativity turns into a product that her organization can market. As personal desires match with organization requirements, people realize that they are most able to gain what they want most by doing what the organization needs most. Assessment 4-1 offers a brief exercise for evaluating the level of employee commitment to and engagement with your organization.

One CEO who wanted to help his company move forward was repeatedly challenged to be "more visionary." This low-key, technically trained engineer confessed to us privately that he would much prefer to outline some concrete goals instead. We could not let him off the hook.

ASSESSMENT 4-1

VOI²C²E employee engagement survey

This survey explores your level of commitment and engagement to your team. Please evaluate the following statements using a ten-point scale on how you perceive your organization today.

Scale: 1 = Low ◄ - - ► 10 = High

Vision: I am proud to work for a company with a clear vision and purpose.	1 2 3 4 5 6 7 8 9 10
Opportunity: I have opportunities to learn and grow.	1 2 3 4 5 6 7 8 9 10
Incentive: My rewards are linked to my performance.	1 2 3 4 5 6 7 8 9 10
Impact: The work I do makes a difference.	1 2 3 4 5 6 7 8 9 10
Community: I work as part of a high-performing team.	1 2 3 4 5 6 7 8 9 10
Communication: I feel like I know what is going on in the organization.	1 2 3 4 5 6 7 8 9 10
Entrepreneurship: I have flexibility in doing my work.	1 2 3 4 5 6 7 8 9 10

Total: _____

After much coaching (and a few threats), he was eventually able to publicly convey his true passion and intensity for the enterprise and its people in his own low-key way. The effect on employees was immediate and positive. They connected with him and with the company in a new way. Had he attempted a vision statement with uncharacteristic hoopla, the result would have been more cynicism that commitment. He was able to find a way to meld his personal strengths with the requirements of the organization in an authentic and congruent way. Leadership hypocrisy exists when you try to be something you are not or behave in a way that is not consistent with your personal style.

One of the most challenging aspects of connecting with the talent your organization requires comes from fully appreciating those who are different from you. Too often we consciously or unconsciously surround ourselves with people like us. We live in neighborhoods with people in our social stratum, our children attend schools with children of similar backgrounds (and we meet with parents of our children's friends), and our social interests generally revolve around those who share professional or personal interests. In reality, talented employees come in any shape, size, age, gender, race, global orientation, personal style—and a host of other factors. You need to be sensitive to the tendency to encircle yourself with people who are like you.

As a talent manager, you need to own the fact that some talent is treated differently from others. While many "historic minorities" often succeed to a certain level in the organization, they may be misplaced for where you really need them today. They may need to be higher up, or in a part of the organization where as minorities they too often don't get to play. Leaders in world-class companies like Goldman Sachs and Deloitte truly live the leadership code when, as leaders taking on tough talent issues, encourage all forms of diversity. At Goldman Sachs, when a talented member of an "out" group does not succeed, top management asks tough questions of the manager involved about the perceived failure. Most particularly, "How would that failure have been perceived had the action, behavior, or results been attached to a member of the 'in' group?" Senior leaders then have the clout to make a difference (diversity trainers do not). The motivation is not just about being fair, or simply about feeling virtuous. In fact, it is about being responsible to shareholders. A well-accepted Catalyst study proves that publicly held corporations with significant numbers of women in the senior leadership ranks (defined as having women as 20 percent of corporate officers) deliver ROE 35 percent higher than that of their peers.[2] It's not that women are better business leaders than men. It's about having a culture and talent systems that are open enough to allow the people with the most to offer to rise to their highest level of contribution, whoever they may be. A similar study needs to be done to measure the effects of other minorities.

When responsibility for accurately managing talent is placed on top executives, be aware that, as well-intentioned as they may be, their perceptions may be limited by their own position, experience, and demographics. To be blunt, top management is often the least aware of these implicit biases. In one organization, the homogeneous top team scored 4.6 (out of a 5.0 scale) to the question, "Are your individual differences treated with dignity and respect?" Their delight was short-lived when shown the responses given by various subgroups: women, minorities, single heads of households, and so forth. It became obvious that the executives didn't know what they didn't know when it came to dealing with diversity. Surveying the members of the "out" groups is a great way to combat this syndrome. Ask these individuals what it is like to work in the organization—they may also have the best ideas for deconstructing the barriers affecting them most directly.

One company we worked with started not by maximizing differences, but by clarifying unity. The CEO and her team determined the handful of key things that every employee at the company had to believe in and act on. These included basic beliefs like serving customers, operating a business at a financial profit, and treating others with respect. They argued that any employee had to know, believe in, and act on these core unifying beliefs. They then said that all other points of view could and should differ and that they would in fact work to encourage differences once they had unity.

STRENGTHEN COMPETENCIES: ENSURE THAT PEOPLE HAVE THE COMPETENCIES THEY NEED

It is clear that leaders need to put the right person in the right job with the right skills at the right time. While an obvious need, it requires that you systematically match the position requirements to the personal competencies of the individual. Defining position requirements begins by examining the outcomes or requirements of a position. An R&D manager must produce a stream of innovative products and services. A marketing manager must deliver revenue from targeted customers. An IT manager must build technology and data systems to help make better decisions. These requirements come from the roles people play in the company and from the expectations placed on those roles. Then, you need to define the competencies required to deliver these outcomes. For an R&D manager to deliver innovation, what knowledge, skills, and abilities must she demonstrate? Creating position clarity with specific competencies required to fill the position enables you to then match individual competencies to position requirements.

With position requirements specified, you may then examine and align an individual's competencies with the position. At the heart of building any employee's competencies lie two questions:

1. What are the employee's personal strengths (competencies, predispositions, abilities)?

2. How can you use or develop these competencies to serve others?

As a leader, you can be a personal coach, mentor, or sponsor or make sure that people recognize and build their competencies and align them to the role they play.

Answering the first question obliges you to help employees recognize what they do well and not so well. Each employee has unique technical and social skills, abilities, and orientations. In orchestrating talent reviews, a CEO we worked with would review the top 3 percent of employees. In this review, he would examine the employees' skills by looking at their education and career backgrounds, their personal interests, and their career successes. While it is dangerous to limit employees to their historical roles, it is helpful to know the talents that employees bring to your organization. In candid conversations with employees, you can help employees uncover blind spots in their skill set.

Responding to the second question suggests matching employees' strengths to the right job or role. The position description lays out requirements and the personal competency assessment suggests opportunities for personal success and growth. Ideally, employees inhabit jobs that not only match their current skills, but will help develop their bandwidth. This may mean offering employees, early in their career, assignments in different industries, countries, or business settings where they can learn and grow. As you resolve to strengthen competencies, you help individuals in your organization grow and develop.

PROVIDE PEOPLE WITH THE RESOURCES TO COPE WITH DEMANDS

A study of teenage depression by clinical psychologist Wendy Ulrich found that the level of resources available to adolescents largely determined their coping ability when faced with high demands.[3] Demands on adolescents include school (grades), work responsibilities, individuating from parents, peer pressures, social responsibilities (like driving), hormones, and personal identity. One might assume that these higher teenage demands lead to teenage depression.

Not so. If resources offset the demands, teenagers stay in balance and cope with the increased expectations. Adolescent resources include parental support, sympathetic peers, helpful teachers and other adults, access to technology, autonomy, control, cognitive ability, and personal talents. Teenagers with high demands but few resources became withdrawn, isolated, and depressed. Yet teens facing similar demands who have access to abundant resources coped and were not depressed. When high resources balance high demands, teenagers are in a productive equilibrium.

In other words, teenagers are human and we can all learn from them. In today's business world, demands are high, including globalization, technology, change, demographics, competition, customers, and financial markets. Few of us can run the thirty- to forty-year career marathon expected today without having it take its toll. Overwork (high demand) leads to burnout, disengagement, short tempers, overeating, sleep deprivation, and a host of chronic illnesses, not to mention strained and broken marriages and alienated children. When overwhelmed by demands, anyone can fall prey to personal depression or career inaction. Employees need resources to cope with these high demands.

Your job as a leader is to recognize and reduce silly demands. For example, don't ask employees to punch time clocks and be visible when the output of their work does not require it. Don't run meetings to hold meetings, set policies that focus on the wrong things, or build complex processes when simple ones will suffice. On the other hand, many business demands are inevitable, and your job is to help employees find resources to cope with those demands.

To get engagement, collaboration, innovation, energy, and productivity from others, find a way to provide them resources to counterbalance the demands (see figure 4-1). There are many resources you can provide employees. Technology enables them to connect with each other and be more productive. Training helps employees learn new ways of thinking and acting that enables them to cope with

FIGURE 4-1

Demand/resource grid

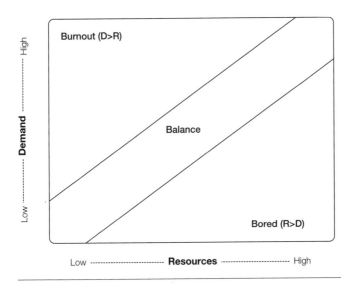

increased demands. Teammates who care for each other offer emotional and social support in the stressful work setting. Autonomy and flexibility over work hours and policies like vacation days and dress help people feel in control of their work and their lives. Research has shown that self-employed people work longer hours, but are more committed to the job primarily because they feel more control over their work conditions. Encouraging members of the organization to devote real time to their outside lives renews the employees' faith in and energy for the company. Make sure that people take their paid vacations, and encourage them to take sufficient time and space during the working day by getting off e-mails and phone calls long enough to get some real work done. Supporting people in improving their diet and exercise habits creates another resource to cope with demands.

As a talent manager, you should resolve to set high expectations on your employees because it stretches them and causes them to grow, but you also have to help them access resources to meet these demands.

CREATE A POSITIVE WORK ENVIRONMENT—PRACTICE SPIRITUAL DISCIPLINES AT WORK

Most of us have worked in environments where negativity, cronyism, fatalism, cynicism, political battles, and narcissism prevail. Few want to stay in these settings, and those who do stay end up being less than fully productive. More time is spent looking inward, protecting themselves, and defending turf instead of identifying and serving customers or investors.

As a leader, you set the tone for how people feel about their work setting, whether it is the corporatewide culture or simply a specific team. Positive psychologists like Martin Seligman assert that people thrive in positive atmospheres where the focus is on what is right, not what is wrong.[4] In their studies of positive psychology, they have delved into the fundamental premises of most of the world's dominant and enduring religions looking for common principles and found that across Hinduism, Buddhism, Judaism, Christianity, Islam, and other religions was an identifiable and enduring set of spiritual disciplines. With a little thought, these notions adapt well to organizational settings. Infusing the workplace with spiritual basics can create a positive work environment.

What are these spiritual basics? First, the wisdom and knowledge that comes from creativity, curiosity, and open-mindedness. The talent-savvy leader helps others learn and grow as well by giving them development opportunities. Second, simple courage: persistence and integrity in the face of difficulties. The leader needs to model a vital bravery in the decisions made and the actions taken. Third: humanity. Build an organization where employees are treated with grace and kindness, where business results occur in a context of humanity and caring, even love. This will be expressed through the fourth spiritual basic of justice, or a universal sense of citizenship and fairness. Related to this is the fifth spiritual basic of temperance: a sense of mercy, humility, and modesty. In a temperate organization, employees can make mistakes and still prosper. Finally, and perhaps above all, the leader can help employees transcend the ordinary by finding greater purpose and meaning in their work. Transcendence finds beauty in the everyday, and comes from a sense of gratitude and hope laced with humor.

These virtues shape an organization that is upbeat and affirming and that supports employee physical and emotional health, productivity, team cohesion, and innovation. As you resolve to model these spiritual disciplines, you can help your talent experience them through your example. When employees experience a positive work environment, they are more likely to stay, be productive, and be an encouraging source for attracting future employees.

HAVE FUN AT WORK

In the midst of six very tough weeks of work, an executive met with his team. As they reviewed the continued earnings loss, the delay in product launches, the ongoing erosion of customer confidence, and the stock declines, the room practically vibrated with the level of stress in it. Despite all the team's hard work, the stream of business setbacks continued. Media reports about their incompetence as a management team only increased the pressure. About thirty minutes into the meeting, the CEO paused and asked, "Are we having fun yet? In the last twenty-four hours, who's had the *worst* business experience?" As they joked about their worst recent experiences, at least some of the tension lifted. With a little gallows humor, the CEO had given his team an emotional reprieve. Such short-term pauses do not remove then challenges leaders face, but they make them easier to face.

Talent managers help people rejuvenate and reenergize. While renewal can come from an energizing vision, or engaging hands-on work, or an uplifting sense of purpose, sometimes it comes from simply having fun. People often need an emotional time-out to let go of stress and let in fresh new ideas. Fun certainly makes working together more of a pleasure and improves morale.

While concepts of fun vary by person, culture, and setting, you can use a variety of techniques to bring fun into the workplace:

- *Humor:* Humor is often person- and time-specific, but when people take even serious subjects with a light touch, they can often do more.

- *Celebrations:* Some leaders find excuses for celebration, including birthdays, holidays, and other key events. Acknowledging key events with merry-making recognizes successes and reinforces them. When these celebrations include customers and extended family members, a work environment may be shaped across boundaries.

- *Events:* Leaders can sponsor events that bring fun into the workplace. These may be in-company events (e.g., town hall meetings), community events (e.g., community service), or special events (e.g., company picnics or Secretary's Day).

- *Contests:* Wisely created contests not only focus attention, but help people organize around a common goal. One executive challenged his team to a contest to find the most useless report generated in the last ninety days. As nominations were made, the team discovered a number of reports that delivered little value.

- *Reward and recognition:* In their work on the "carrot principle," Adrian Gostick and Chester Elton demonstrate that recognition programs can be used to shape employee behavior. They have extensively studied how leaders can reward and recognize good performance as a way to reinforce good performance.[5] They offer over one hundred ideas for recognizing employees (e.g., business trips, personal notes, etc.) that help employees feel appreciated for the work that they do.

- *Symbols:* One executive who was a devoted Duke Blue Devil alumnus started the "blue devil award"; employees who performed exceptional work would receive a stuffed blue devil with an appreciation note from the executive. These personal awards become symbols of executive attention for good performance and were prized among the recipients.

- *Personal self-deprecation*: Some leaders take themselves very seriously and have great pride in their role and status. Others, while accepting the duties of their role, approach their tasks with humility. They readily share successes and are willing to acknowledge their weaknesses.

- *Fitness centers:* Team and individual athletic events may help employees gain energy. Sponsoring teams, building fitness centers, and encouraging physical well-being may help employees find more pleasure at work.

- *Concierge services:* Some companies offer employees who work long hours concierge services. These services may include help with life's routines (dry cleaning, tickets and reservations, and other support). By offering these services at work, companies make it possible for employees to stay more focused on the work they need to do.

Leaders who resolve to bring fun into the workplace do not make light of serious business issues, but they create a work environment that encourages people to be productive.

NO ONE IN TODAY'S INTERNET AGE and knowledge economy would deny the importance of talent. Good talent is the source of ideas. But finding, engaging, and retaining talent requires that you learn to nurture and develop others. To do so comes from knowing and applying the resolutions we have suggested. The general rule is that when you feel as much pride in and respect for the lives and successes of others as they do for themselves you will inspire more goodwill and loyalty in others. The result is increased personal satisfaction with work, commitment to work, and productivity to better do the work.

Go to www.leadershipcodebook.com for a video of Dave Ulrich more fully explaining how to approach these talent resolutions and be a better talent manager.

Rule 4

Build the Next Generation

To build the next generation, be a *human capital developer*:

1. Map the workforce.
2. Create a firm and employee brand.
3. Help people manage their careers.
4. Find and develop next-generation talent.
5. Encourage networks and relationships.

HUMAN CAPITAL DEVELOPERS invest in the next generation of talent. Today's talent matters, but tomorrow's talent matters just as much. Leaders who invest in tomorrow's talent build for the future, create sustainability, and ensure a legacy. Human capital should be enhanced just as financial, information, and relationship capital are. As you prepare tomorrow's talent, you will come to recognize and respond to challenges of retiring baby boomers, N-Gen, and the rise of global talent from places like China and India. Ultimately, your success as a leader is the extent to which you have built leadership, or the next generation of leaders. Effective leaders ultimately make others more effective.

In this regard, leaders who develop human capital are like good parents who devote enormous energy to increasing their children's opportunities. Good parents offer children opportunities to learn and grow in ways that enhance each child's unique personality. They encourage and coach them to reach their full potential. They delight in the success of their children, and pass onto the next generation an improved quality of life. Effective leaders do the same with their employees. They help employees learn and grow by coaching, supporting, and delighting in employees' successes. One of your primary leadership roles is to cultivate next-generation employees.

In thinking about future talent, "war for talent" is the overused analogy; but it is wrong, because it is too bound up in zero-sum game imagery where there are winners and losers. One child does not have to fail for another to succeed. Each child can succeed by developing his or her unique gifts. Likewise, leaders who foster next-generation talent engage in a purposeful crusade (not war) founded on values that engage hearts and minds and that create win/win, not win/lose, solutions. Success comes from helping individual employees excel in their specific assignments by helping them identify and develop their gifts. Human capital developers commit that future talent will be prepared for future opportunities. They work to match today's people with tomorrow's positions to ensure sustainability of organization success. You can ensure your legacy if you live up to five pledges we suggest. We like the *pledge* metaphor because it has a future orientation, about what talent can be, not just what it is today.

MAP THE WORKFORCE

Success requires having the right people in the right places at the right time with the right skills. Once the strategy is clear, map out the key positions and identify people to fill them. Such mapping requires differentiation of both people and positions. Some positions (roles, tasks, responsibilities) in a company generate more customer share and economic revenue than others. Some people have greater or less ability to meet business results. Differentiation of people and positions requires not only leadership courage to make difficult distinctions, but insights as to criteria for key positions and people.

Critical Jobs. Critical jobs go by many names—key positions, wealth-creating jobs, A positions, and others. Critical jobs are those wealth-creating jobs that are critical to the firm's growth, the particular jobs that really impact the success of company. In technology firms, critical jobs may be research positions pursuing innovation through R&D; in retail firms, critical jobs may be front-line positions driving the customer experience in investment firms, critical jobs may be technical positions offering some rare insights about the financial markets; in emerging markets, critical jobs may be marketing jobs requiring local expertise; and so forth. Identify these key positions and place and develop your best talent in these positions.

One of our colleagues, Dick Beatty, uses the example of airline pilots to point out that critical jobs are not always the obvious choices. Ask yourself: when you select your flight, do you do it because of the quality of the pilot? No. You choose based on the responsiveness of the gate agent, or the on-time record that is primarily a function of the professionalism of the ground crew. Customers care about making easy reservations, getting to their destinations on time, getting the best fare, and, in the case of Southwest Airlines, perhaps hearing a joke from a flight attendant that makes them forget about the crowded conditions in coach. They assume that pilots in every airline have equal technological skill at flying safely. The differential jobs are those that affect customer decision making.

For the jobs that really count, you will need the best possible talent who are capable of differentiating the firm in the mind of its key customers. Getting the best talent comes by setting clear standards about what is expected and then sourcing, screening, and securing potential employees (who likely have choices to work elsewhere) and orienting and engaging them in their jobs.

For example, imagine you want to grow through product innovation. With this strategic clarity, you can think about what the core technical competencies of your organization are. Critical jobs will likely be those that drive your technical core competencies. In this case, the critical jobs might be key positions as software designers who are charged with creating new product or services. Part of this team might be in Central Europe, another part in the United States, and a third somewhere in Southeast Asia. To staff this team, you have to source future employees who are technically able to design products, but you also have to source individuals who know how to collaborate and connect and communicate despite the separations of time and distance, as well as language, culture, custom, ethnicity, and, perhaps, gender. The best workers in the future will need to have technical competencies *and* social capabilities that well exceed those of previous generations.

These rare people will be worth their weight in gold. Your workforce plan will identify these critical positions and then build an approach to sourcing, securing, and orienting the right individuals into those key positions.

In figure 5-1, you can see that different roles provide different levels of value for the organization. So, all work can be divided into three types of work (and jobs):

1. Critical jobs

2. Support roles work

3. Nonessential work

Typically only about 10 to 20 percent of the workforce is engaged in true wealth-creating roles. Most very senior

FIGURE 5-1

All jobs are not created equal

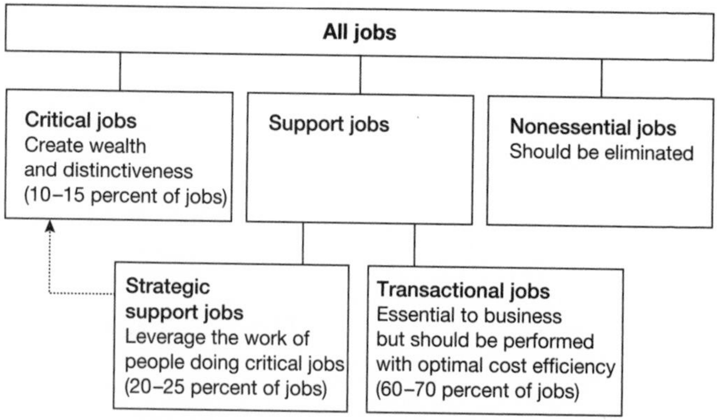

executive roles should be on this critical jobs list because of their potential for impact on large numbers of people. However, critical jobs can also be found in much more junior roles. For example, the barista at a Starbucks has a critical job because she is the person who creates the experience for the customer. The process control engineer in a manufacturing company has a critical job because of the impact this job has on production and uptime. Other jobs in the organization support the people doing these critical jobs or should be done at optimal cost efficiencies to allow the organization to stay in business. Strategic support jobs leverage the ability of people doing the critical work to do what they do more effectively. Transactional work jobs are more routine but they are essential to the organization and provide cost efficiencies.

Key Questions. As a leader, you should be asking three sets of questions to match position and person:

1. Which critical jobs will make the largest difference to your results in the next five to ten years? If you don't know, how can you find out?

2. How well positioned are you to staff those critical jobs with the right people? What percent of the key positions are staffed by people who are

qualified for the future? What percent of those who are fully qualified are at risk of moving?

3. What percent of the key positions have qualified talent in place? What is your *back-up ratio* (the number of people qualified to move into key positions divided by key positions)?

When you put A players in A positions, you are likely to deliver on business outcomes that matter most and likely to help your best talent be engaged in creating your future. If you put A players in C positions where they cannot impact business results, you are likely to lose your A players, since they may have opportunities elsewhere. If you put a C player in an A position, you will likely miss business opportunities. The matrix in figure 5-2 can help you match talent to positions.

FIGURE 5-2

Critical jobs matrix

	Positions			
Players		A	B	C
	A			
	B			
	C			

You also need to acknowledge that the crusade for human capital has more complex workforce demographics than ever before. Gender, age, education, and global mix will all shape the employees you require for your future strategy. When you spend time thinking about these demographic issues you will be more able to get the best and brightest. Too often, leaders live in exclusive ghettos surrounded both at work and at home by those who look and act like them. They are not sensitive to the unique demands or expectations of those who differ from them but who comprise the workforce of the future.

Your pledge should be to have a workforce plan with key positions and people for your organization that reflects your strategy. You should regularly require and review workforce plans as frequently as you review strategy and organization plans.

CREATE A FIRM AND EMPLOYEE BRAND

Distinctive firm brands become important stakeholders: customers or clients, investors, the community, and, most importantly for this discussion, employees. Related to the firm brand is an employee brand: how the identity of the firm, in effect, makes promises to its employees. A strong employee brand sends messages to current and future employees about what they should expect from their employment with the firm. As a result of the brand, employees may self-select to not join a firm. For example, an applicant at Disney who does not find joy in serving disheveled and stressed guests with a smile and helpful greeting would not do well. A high roller would not make it at Wal-Mart.

As you show interest in future talent you need to think carefully through your firm's employee brand. What do you want to promise employees who work at your company? What should these employees expect from you? When employees do good work, what do they get in return? How will your firm distinguish itself as a place to work for the most talented employees who have lots of choices about where they could work? What will entice the best employees to come to work for you? What will make your employees proud that they have chosen to work in your firm? What do you want them to tell their friends and associates about working with you? You don't need to answer these questions alone, but you should make sure that you have answers. In finding answers, start by asking parallel questions about customers. The brand metaphor works because your firm's identity with customers should mimic your identity with employees. Nestlé's slogan, "Good food; good life," implies that its employees should maintain a healthy lifestyle (nutrition, diet, exercise) to embody the firm's commitment to food and life.

You need to look carefully at yourself to see if you embody and live the employee brand you articulate. You need to become the exemplar, the icon, of what you want others to do. If you say you want creativity, your behaviors and actions need to be unique and creative. If you say you are serious about efficiency, you need to be thrifty in your choices. Nothing destroys an employee brand more quickly than leadership hypocrisy. If you don't live what you ask of others, they won't live with you.

By building an employee brand, you make a pledge or promise to present and future employees about how they should expect to be treated when they do good work.

HELP PEOPLE MANAGE THEIR CAREERS

Developing future employees often requires helping an employee have a sense of his own personal career opportunities and the future needs of the corporation. When we teach expensive two- or four-week executive programs at the University of Michigan, we find that fewer than 20 percent of those who attend (at great company and personal cost) have *not* had a career conversation about how this program fits with their career interests. What a waste!

Building human capital requires you to have candid, forward-looking, and helpful conversations with employees about what they want and what they can expect from their careers. Too often, leaders don't talk to their employees about their career and performance for a variety of reasons—for example, they don't want to raise expectations about a specific job or they don't want to argue about things they can't control. Just as typically, they don't have a framework and language to talk about career development in a useful way, especially to professional employees.

Career Stages. To facilitate career conversations, we suggest a model we have developed building on the work of Gene Dalton and Paul Thompson that describes four stages in a professional's development.[1] This model helps you, as a human capital developer, enable development opportunities for individuals in the organization as well as identify organization-level development gaps in the talent pipeline (see figure 5-3 for a graphic representation of these stages).

The career development model helps the professional define his or her career aspirations and understand what is required for high performance where they are now. It articulates how the stages and the tracks differ in the tasks that the professionals are expected to perform, in the types

FIGURE 5-3

The RBL Group stages of development

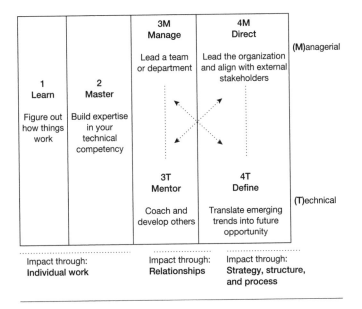

		3M Manage Lead a team or department	4M Direct Lead the organization and align with external stakeholders	(M)anagerial
1 Learn Figure out how things work	2 Master Build expertise in your technical competency			
		3T Mentor Coach and develop others	4T Define Translate emerging trends into future opportunity	(T)echnical

Impact through:
Individual work

Impact through:
Relationships

Impact through:
**Strategy, structure,
and process**

of relationships they form, and in the psychological adjustments they must make.

In stage I, employees are dependent, working under the direction of others, helping and learning from more experienced people who may serve as bosses, mentors, or coaches. Work is never entirely independent but rather comprises assignments that are portions of a larger project actively overseen by a more senior professional. The stage I performer is expected to willingly do the detailed and routine work of the team.

In stage II, the employees demonstrate their competence as independent contributors. They go in-depth into one problem or technical area and assume responsibility for a definable portion of a project, process, or client. They develop credibility and a reputation as an expert, and they use their burgeoning confidence to develop more of their own interior and exterior resources to succeed on the job.

Whether on a technical or managerial track, by the time employees get to stage III, these professionals are involved enough in their own work to make significant technical contributions while beginning to expand beyond their technical expertise. Stage III professionals stimulate others through ideas and information, and help to develop others in the role of idea leader, mentor, or team leader or manager.

The few employees who make it to stage IV provide direction for the organization, exercising formal and informal power to initiate action and influence decisions. They may represent the organization inside and outside its boundaries, and are in a position to act as sponsors for other employees, helping to prepare them for key roles in the organization. While many organizations don't require a stage IV technical role, an organization with a strong need for technology contributions likely has a few stage IV technical employees who create significant competitive advantage for the firm.

This model helps frame productive career development discussions with employees that are not about individual jobs but are about the overall architecture of a career. It also helps employees assess their current stage, and helps them to figure out whether they want to move to the next stage, another track in the stage they are currently in, or remain highly valued where they are. A knowledge worker who stays current with changes in his or her field can remain valued by staying in any stage except stage I for an entire career. The value of the stages model is its ability to help people recognize the trade-offs inherent in changing the type and level of their contribution to the organization.

As you help people recognize and work on their careers, you can identify possible gaps in the talent pipeline for your organization. You might find, for example, that there are too few future store managers for your organization to expand as rapidly as you would like. You might recognize that a disproportionate percentage of people in a given job category or stage are eligible to retire in the near future, leaving you with a serious talent gap.

As you help people make sense of their career choices and opportunities and as you build a talent pipeline within your organization, you pledge to employees that they will have opportunities available to them if they meet certain milestones.

FIND AND DEVELOP
NEXT-GENERATION TALENT

By this point it is probably obvious that everyone in the organization needs to be a talent scout, to be constantly on the lookout for great young talent. Everyone should be seeking great talent with the logic of the workforce map in mind. We believe that the best source of future talent is present talent. When we ask executives in seminars, "Do you know of someone today who would be a good employee at your company?" generally 80 percent of them respond with a clear yes. Through social and professional contacts, they know someone who would do a good job at the company. When we then ask, "How many of you have a disciplined process for contacting these potential future employees and inviting them to join your company?" almost no one responds. For critical positions, you can source future talent by inviting current talent to make recommendations. Of course, you need to manage diversity and assure that you don't just hire mirror images of present employees. And, even more important, when current talent recommends future talent, the current talent becomes more committed. In a grocery store, we seldom change lines when someone gets in line behind us. If a top talent is instrumental in attracting a future employee, the referring employee is much less likely to leave. This is a win/win. You can identify and attract great talent and engage and retain current top talent by involving current employees in sourcing future employees.

And when you find and bring the right talent into your organization, be relentless in pursuit of it. Once you've caught it, don't let it go. Coaching and mentoring help people know what to do to fit in and succeed. Delegating and empowering builds both individual and organizational muscle, and is another way for the organization to develop people while also showing confidence in them.

Talk with current talent about what they want. Beverly Kaye, in her book *Love 'Em or Lose 'Em: Getting Good People to Stay*, has a simple but profound idea called the "stay interview." For talented employees, you can simply find time to talk with them to tell them you appreciate their work (which is very reinforcing), and ask them what they need to stay with the firm. Generally not a part of the formal appraisal process, this conversation conveys value and appreciation to the employee, and gives valuable information about how to keep them.[2] The simple act of listening to their needs and concerns gives them an outlet for any stress they may be feeling, and can defuse any incipient need to move on.

As a human capital developer, your legacy will come because you invested in future talent. You found the right ones, helped them perform well in current and future jobs, and helped make your company an attractive place to work.

Coach and Mentor. It is a truism that people generally don't quit companies, they quit bosses. Connecting the talent slated for the A positions is especially important, and that connection needs to extend beyond their current boss.

One of the best ways to care for such employees—and to let them know that the organization values them for the long run—is to give them a formal coach. That coach could be internal to the organization, or could be an external consultant. Coaches might help future employees in both upgrading behaviors and delivering results. Behavior coaching helps future talent learn the choices and consequences of their behaviors. For example, how they will be regarded if they are too loud—or too soft-spoken? Results coaching helps recent hires with potential to be clear about outcomes they will need to be able to point to as they progress: the jobs they need to cycle through to get the experience and visibility they need for promotion. This kind of guidance is valuable for everyone. It is especially critical for women and other minorities who are less likely to have an existing network that helps to steer them toward the right jobs and experiences.

Most successful people also had a mentor (or mentors) at critical points in their career. Someone has to help a younger employee steer through the organizational dynamics (otherwise known as politics). The right mentor can also give the talent the visibility she needs to be considered for the right positions as succession plans are drawn.

Delegate and Empower. An accomplished executive credits much of her success to bosses and mentors who gave her challenging assignments very early on—assignments for which she was not truly qualified to take on at the time, like managing a complex project, working on a difficult customer assignment, building a business in a foreign country, and so forth. She valued these assignments highly because her mentors' confidence in her buoyed her confidence in herself, and she was able to learn from successes and failures she would otherwise not have had.

As her coaches, we asked her if she was providing similar opportunities to stretch to the next generation. As she thought about it, she realized she was not. Big assignments carried big risks, and she feared that talented but inexperienced employees would make mistakes that could cost the company reputation and financial return. So, she would often intervene and keep potential future leaders from making bad decisions. This is a leadership danger sign. She needed to do for others what her bosses had done for her.

If you want to build effective human capital, you will need to delegate, empower, and allow employees to take risks, even if they occasionally fail, as long as they learn. Delegation means that you give an employee clear tasks, with definitive outcomes, accountabilities, and resources to do the task. When an employee comes to you with questions about a project, often the best response is, "What do you think?" More often than not, the employee has considered alternatives, and may just be waiting to be asked to recommend a course of action. Probe for ideas, and you'll discover that these employees will make the right decision 80 percent of the time. When their judgment is wrong, your job is to help them examine how they came to the wrong decision so they can learn a process for decision making. Delegation is about coaching and teaching, not judging and evaluating.

Empowerment means giving your employees knowledge, authority, and incentives to make good decisions. If you give an employee the authority to make a decision, but do not give him the information to make the right decision, you have entrapped, not empowered, that employee. To empower, you need to share information as well as authority. When one of our children got his driver's license, he had authority to drive. But his father did not give him enough information about driving in icy conditions, so in the first ice storm, he had a minor accident.

The father's first instinct was to blame him for reckless driving, but he realized that he had given his son authority without information, which is a dangerous combination. As a leader, make sure you empower people by giving them both authority and information.

Share Incentives. Finally, share incentives. Employees know that senior executives and high-performing individuals should get paid more. But when the gap between their personal compensation and the compensation of senior executives gets too high (a recent study showed that, in the United States, the CEO's total compensation was over two hundred times that of the first-line supervisor), who can blame employees for feeling embittered, not empowered?

Your pledge to employees who will be in your company when you are gone is to give them opportunities to learn and grow so that they are prepared when their leadership opportunities arise.

ENCOURAGE NETWORKS AND RELATIONSHIPS

We all know that having a friend at work is one of the main reasons to stay and to work hard. As a leader, you can help foster a supportive community of colleagues where people work together in the moment, but also have an emotional tie to the organization. Communities of practice, for example, are especially helpful in attracting and retaining talented women and other historic minorities since they have traditionally lacked networks that can help them to advance in corporations. Strong networks also lead to faster learning and more collaboration.

Some companies, including Ernst & Young, McDonald's, and the CIA, use social networking spaces like Facebook, Nexopia, or Friendster to help their people network. The sites operate as a storehouse for living résumés that employees can update themselves as they gain experience, and as a virtual job fair where internal jobs and internal candidates can meet. Ketchum has developed what it terms a "transparent, fluid internal job market" in which "boomerangs" (people who have left and come back) are just as valuable as people who stay.

Your pledge to future employees is that the social setting of work will encourage collaboration more than competition, friendships more than rivalries, and connection more than isolation.

PROUD PARENTS REVEL in the maturation and success of their children. As a leader of human capital, you pledge that the next generation of employees will be stronger than the present. When you do this, you gain a reputation as an outstanding developer of future talent. You create workforce plans that match key positions to top talent; create a firm and employee brand, help people manage their careers, find and develop next-generation talent, and encourage networks and relationships. As a result, the organization you someday leave will be in better shape than the one you entered, a simple test for a human capital developer.

On www.leadershipcodebook.com, Paul Thompson, the original author of the stages work, joins *Leadership Code* coauthor Norm Smallwood to give a complete introduction to the framework as well as practical advice for applying it. Also try your hand at a number of mini-cases about stages, and take the premium full stages assessment tool.

Rule 5

Invest in Yourself

To invest in yourself, be *personally proficient*:

1. Practice clear thinking: rise above the details.

2. Know yourself.

3. Tolerate stress.

4. Demonstrate learning agility.

5. Tend to your own character and integrity.

6. Take care of yourself.

7. Have personal energy and passion.

PERSONAL PROFICIENCY IS THE ULTIMATE rule of leadership, and it starts by knowing yourself. If you are not grounded through your values and beliefs, credible through your judgment, emotionally mature through your ability to analyze yourself and connect with others, and willing to learn and grow as a leader, you will not be prepared to be a strategist, executor, talent manager, or human capital developer. Who you are becomes a key predictor of what you can help others to become. When you have personal insights into yourself, you will be more able to lead others.

We call this broad leadership rule *personal proficiency* because it is about you and your personal qualifications to lead others. Personal proficiency comes from knowing your predispositions, strengths, and weaknesses. It is about extracting important lessons from your life experiences and applying them with care, discernment, energy, courage, and humanity. It requires equal measures of self-awareness and self-discipline—a certain quality of mindfulness in going about the intertwined businesses of life and work. It requires having the courage to be bold and take risks while still having the humility to learn from and share credit with others. In some ways, personal proficiency is the most difficult rule to train or develop. Some leaders are more innately gifted in the personal insights that lead to proficiency, but for all, we can delineate specific recommendations that will help you gain insights into yourself and lead you to become more personally proficient.

PRACTICE CLEAR THINKING: RISE ABOVE THE DETAILS

Clear thinking is a combination of intellect and intuition, reason and emotion. A marketing executive received a large book of customer data detailing customer attitudes by product, geography, customer size, and other dimensions, all parsed to a very subtle level of nuance. Studying the data with the intention not of mastering every detail but of finding patterns, she identified three themes. These themes allowed her to set priorities that soon drove decisions and actions. Clear thinking requires getting past the details to see the broader implications and thus exercise good judgment. In this sense, she was like the chess master who sees the strategy, not just the moves. A good chess player who is asked to replace all the pieces on the chess board thirty moves into a game often tries to memorize where each piece is located and can only replace a small percentage of the individual pieces. The chess *master*, after thirty moves, sees a pattern to the game and can replace all the pieces according to the pattern. When learning to type, we learn the letters, but fast typists type words or phrases because they work with words, not letters. To see patterns and not get lost in details, you need to learn to frame problems conceptually and communicate broader objectives. You need to master the principles and allow others to determine the practices that will help them deliver on the principles.

Leaders who think clearly can quickly set priorities and act on them. In a classic role-play called *The In-Box*, executives have thirty minutes to deal with an impossible number of items in a fictitious inbox. The best leaders quickly scan all the items and focus on the top few that deserve their attention (like the memo from the government threatening to shut down their operation in twenty-four hours). A large number of executives race to act, feverishly working through each item in order, and fail to uncover the priority item (often buried deep in the in-box), let alone deal with it. Top leaders transcend the pressure—they simply act, keep their cool, and focus on what matters most.

Leaders who think clearly also do not shy away from the toughest decisions. One senior leader jokingly lamented, "I get blamed for a lot of wrong decisions because I am given the tough problems. If a problem has an 80 percent obvious solution, I should not be dealing with it. I get the 51/49 problems that are messy, ambiguous, and not clear-cut." Yet, even when solutions are not obvious, you need to be able to face and make the tough decisions. Asking and reminding yourself and others, "What is the decision that has to be made?" helps you focus attention on the decision that needs to be made rather than getting lost in the details. Even with 51/49 problems, you need to act with 90/10 decisiveness.

Proceed with Courage and Boldness. Clear thinking needs decisive action. Take the shot. Inevitably, the top basketball players want the ball when the game is on the line. They are willing to take the responsibility of taking the final shot. One leading professional player has the mantra "No guts, no glory" tattooed on his arms. Bold leadership is no different. If there is a decision to make, identify it, study it, and make it. If you're wrong, admit it and learn, but be willing to act.

Courageous and bold leaders have personal confidence and security. They make mistakes, but learn from them. Companies with a blue ocean strategy have first-mover advantages because they define new markets. Leaders who act with boldness and courage also have first-mover advantage because they make things happen rather than watch what has happened.

KNOW YOURSELF

We coached a CEO who rose to the top of his organization in part because of his low-key approach to connecting with employees, customers, and others. Smart, analytical, and a lifelong introvert, he led effectively within the company through one-on-one conversations, e-mails, structured meetings, and formal events. Then the competitive situation changed. As the performance problems mounted, the investment community, local community, and other stakeholders clamored for a visible public face for the company. Deeply passionate about the survival of his company, the CEO set aside his predisposition to hunker down in his office and instead went public. To become the public face of the company, he had to share himself—who he was, what he thought, and how he spent his time. In so doing, he conveyed his rock-solid confidence that the firm would succeed. For two months, this modest man did media interviews and met with suppliers, regulators, customers, community leaders, and trade unions. He became the public face of his company. While he became adept in his public expressions, he was never completely comfortable with it. But his competence and passion overcame his predisposition, and he learned while he did what was required to help his company succeed.

This leader knew himself: what he was good at, what he was not good at, and what he needed to change because of what mattered most to him. As you honestly reflect on who you are and who you need to be, you can create greater leadership bandwidth to respond to business conditions and resolve to do the right thing. Assessment 6-1 offers an exercise for you to look at your personal proficiency strengths and weaknesses. Figure 6-1 shows a sample "radar"—a quick graphic to help you see your personal proficiency profile.

ASSESSMENT 6-1

Personal proficiency test

Personal proficiency comes from investing in yourself. The following diagnostic identifies some of the key skills and behaviors of those who demonstrate personal proficiency. You might use this for a self-assessment or have others rate you on these dimensions for a more complete picture. You might also take the more comprehensive assessment online at www.leadershipcodebook.com.

To what extent to you . . .   Scale: 1 = Low ◄ - - ► 10 = High

1. Focus on a few critical issues	1 2 3 4 5 6 7 8 9 10
2. See patterns in data	1 2 3 4 5 6 7 8 9 10
3. Know what you like and are good at	1 2 3 4 5 6 7 8 9 10
4. Work at what you need to do but don't necessarily enjoy doing	1 2 3 4 5 6 7 8 9 10
5. Ask for feedback and observations about yourself	1 2 3 4 5 6 7 8 9 10
6. Remain calm under stress	1 2 3 4 5 6 7 8 9 10
7. Seek new ideas or ways of solving problems	1 2 3 4 5 6 7 8 9 10
8. Learn from experiences by improving on the past	1 2 3 4 5 6 7 8 9 10
9. Look out for others as well as for yourself	1 2 3 4 5 6 7 8 9 10
10. Take care physically (nutrition, exercise, sleep, meditation)	1 2 3 4 5 6 7 8 9 10
11. Take care socially (support network of trusted colleagues and friends)	1 2 3 4 5 6 7 8 9 10
12. Feel passion about your work	1 2 3 4 5 6 7 8 9 10

Scoring: **Total:_____**

50–60 = Excellent; 43–49 = Good; 36–42 = Fair; below 35 = Poor—take better care of yourself

FIGURE 6-1

Personal proficiency graph (sample)

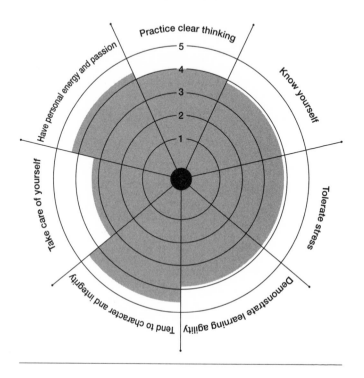

Understand Your Predispositions. When one of us was heavy, he thought he could avoid the problem by simply not looking in a mirror. Turns out, he was wrong. To stay healthy, he had to step on the scale every day and accept the tough challenges of diet and exercise. He had to look in the mirror and see reality. He is not alone. Research has shown that people can often see their strengths, but have a much harder time assessing their weaknesses.

To be personally proficient, you must begin by looking in the leadership mirror and being honest with yourself about your full range of personal predispositions: the good, the bad, and the ugly, as the saying goes. The more you understand your predispositions—to be introverted or extroverted, to seek risk or to avoid it, to work with people or with data, to work with ideas or take action, to be patient or impatient, and so on—the more you can own your reality and work to adapt it.

Your personal insights should liberate, not limit, you. Understanding predispositions is not about putting yourself in a box, but about helping you understand the contours of your current field of play. Being good at, say, analytics should not necessarily mean you can only be the numbers guy. Being less comfortable with interpersonal skills does not mean you can never learn to build a strong, cohesive team. Predispositions are simply starting points. One of us is strongly predisposed to being an introvert. Given a choice, he would work alone in his office, blissfully relieved of social obligations. Yet he is a teacher by trade, a job that requires engaging classrooms full of people for hours at a time. While predisposed to introversion, he has learned to "do" extroversion.

How do you discover your predispositions? Start by checking your own gut. What work is easy, energizing, and enjoyable? What work comes naturally? What activities on your to-do list do you go for first? What work challenges do you love? Positive psychologist Martin Seligman calls these your signature strengths—the things you both like doing and are good at. His advice: go with them.[1] Of course, when you identify your strengths you can also identify what does not come naturally. Doing things that are easy, energizing, and enjoyable come naturally to you, but you also have to do what is exigent to do so that your business will succeed. Having identified and defined it, you can now begin to be specific about how to improve—like the CEO who became the public face of his company, who was able to apply his analytical bias to improving his media and public relationship skills. Sometimes, you can apply your strengths to the areas you need to improve.

Continue to know yourself by asking those who know you best for candid observations about your talents and behaviors. As a senior leader, it is far too easy to let yourself be surrounded by yes-men and -women who try to ingratiate themselves with you by not giving you honest feedback. Seek out true allies who will tell you how they see you, and who will also share ideas about how to improve. Both honest conversations and 360-degree assessments can help here.

You might also learn through any number of personal audits. These surveys can help you to identify your leadership style in greater detail, and often provide good, highly specific ideas for what to do differently if the business situation requires new skills to come to the fore. Recognize, however, that moving beyond your natural predispositions will take a lot of energy and constant vigilance, at least at first. Being curious about and observing your leadership predispositions will help you know where to focus to be personally proficient.

The real goal of knowing yourself is to connect signature strengths and passions to work demands. You need to build on your strengths *that strengthen others*. Making sure that your actions mesh with passions builds your self-confidence, but using your strengths to help others builds their confidence in you and lets you lead. You can be asking the related questions: Do I build on my strengths? Do I use my strengths to strengthen others?

TOLERATE STRESS

Unless you have achieved a rare state of Zen mastery, chances are that you will find the working world stressful. The removal of work and life boundaries through Black-Berrys, e-mail, and constant contact; the hours we work; and the promises we strive to keep to customers, colleagues, and ourselves inevitably take their toll in the form of stress. Many days, nothing seems easy, especially dealing with the ambiguities and complexities inherent in the corporate world.

One of the greatest sources of stress for ambitious people is fear of failure. Courageous and bold leaders take risks, and sometimes those risks don't work out. We have learned a simple formula for risk taking: will to win divided by fear of failure. Increasing the will to win comes as you feel a personal passion, desire to succeed, and believe in the outcomes of your agenda. Reducing fear of failure comes as organizations build in career and compensation safety nets to buffer against mistakes.

Successful leaders recover quickly from setbacks. Their emotional resilience springs from two sources. One, a general sense of optimism: "It didn't work last time but it will next time." The second is a tendency to externalize the failure. By that we mean that they are able to see that the failure came from the context and conditions—the market, say, or a weakness in the supply chain—rather than from themselves. People who lack resilience immediately blame themselves—their very worth as humans—when something goes wrong. They quit. People with resilience are willing to shrug off setbacks, learn from the situation, and move on.

Since being a leader means managing the emotions and expectations of others as well as oneself, it is critical to maintain composure even in extremely difficult circumstances. We all know people who "lose it" when the going gets tough. These are the folks who start pointing fingers as soon as something goes wrong. Effective leaders remain in control of their emotions when it counts.

DEMONSTRATE LEARNING AGILITY

For you to take your organization in a new direction, you need to be curious. You should see the world not only as it is, but as it can be. You should want to know more about the outside (markets, the competition)—and the inside (what is happening in your organizations, how it could be better). Our colleagues Bob Eichinger and Mike Lombardo found that leaders who learn quickly and well, and who perpetually apply new ideas to current problems succeed not only in the short term but over the long haul. They call this trait "learning agility."[2] Successful leaders value learning so highly that they insist others do it too. This bent toward learning is often innate, yet can also be acquired.

Be Willing to Generalize from the Past. Analyze what you have done in the past. Do not just look at what worked or did not work, but explore why. Recognize significant events that happened, but look for patterns. Many organizations get locked into ways of doing things that limit the ability to learn. We have identified what we call *viruses*—dysfunctional patterns that stifle learning and creativity. What are viruses? Things such as deference to authority, activity mania, ambiguous accountability, slavish devotion to numbers, and so forth (see chapter 3 for a fuller discussion). You can ask your direct reports about what viruses have infected how your team works. We have found that once these viruses are identified, named, and exposed, they can usually be inoculated and eventually cured.

Looking back should allow you to move forward differently. Keep looking in your leadership mirror to see what you have done, but look beyond it to see what you should do. Constantly try to understand how to improve performance and avoid making the same mistakes twice. Failing is not failing if it leads to learning. Keep looking for feedback, really reflect on it, and be resilient.

Seek New Ideas. Look for new ways to try to solve old problems. You can put yourself in the path of new ideas and learning opportunities by reading, talking with others, and paying attention to new information outside of the usual sources. Experiment with new ways of doing things. Surround yourself with people who see the world differently from you. Benchmark best practices in your industry and outside your industry so that you can leapfrog them. Be disciplined about continuous improvement through initiatives like Six Sigma, lean, or simplicity. Test yourself periodically to make sure that your ideas are evolving. In presentations to key customers, investors, or employees, make sure that you are continually proposing fresh ideas.

Be Unique and Creative. Ask questions that probe for alternatives. Find a balance between analytics grounded in data and intuition rooted in instinct. Data ensures that decisions are logical and consistent with past patterns. Instinct means that you do what you sense is right even if the data does not confirm your decision. If you can combine both data and instinct in the decisions you make, you will recognize old patterns, but build new ones. Such clear thinking requires not only an intellectual quotient (IQ) and an emotional or social quotient (EQ or SQ), but also a *clarity quotient* (CQ) to create confidence in the direction.

Avoid Extremes. In practice, even the most aggressive and action-oriented leaders avoid extremes and thus remain credible. To avoid extremes, stay connected to others. Leadership, after all, is a team sport, and spending too much time alone cuts off ideas and engagement. Moving ahead with bold actions requires that your plans be vetted and tested with the people who will understand how the actions might play out—they may even be responsible for executing on them. Avoiding extremes also means sharing credit. Confident, accomplished, and successful leaders accustomed to the limelight need to be open to the possibilities of learning from others. Respecting the contributions of others not only leads to great ideas, but also helps others to take pride in their work. Finally, being a leader does not mean never having to say you're sorry. Even CEOs, presidents, and senior executives make mistakes. Admit them. Leaders who try to hide or run from their mistakes spend more energy covering themselves than finding workable solutions. As an added benefit, leaders who acknowledge weaknesses and 'fess up to their mistakes may find their imperfect humanity endears them to others more than fake invincibility.

Consider the case of Chuck Prince, CEO of financial giant Citigroup from 2003 to 2007, when he resigned over the subprime mortgage scandal. He "grew up" in the world of mergers and acquisitions, a talented lawyer brought along by Sandy Weill, a force of nature in the M&A world. The challenge Prince faced as CEO was in many ways the exact opposite of what he had accomplished to get there: the office of the CEO of Citigroup during Prince's tenure was no longer about buying businesses and attaching them to the mother ship through financial reporting, but was instead about skillfully knitting together the global patchwork of Citigroup's many businesses into an integrated enterprise. This new objective required creating integrating structures, systems, politics, and cultures, but in five years as CEO, Prince made virtually little impact in those areas. Prince failed in large part because he did not learn new ways of approaching the business. Why? Because he continued to rely on the same people who got him there, when what he needed was to be surrounded by people who could help him see new ways of doing things and develop new strategic patterns. As a consequence, he could only do what he knew how to do. In a changing world, that is the surest path to failure.

Create a Learning Cycle. Combine all four of the above steps into a learning cycle. The cycle would look something like this:

1. *Choice:* Expand your range of choices by looking back, planning forward, experimenting, and surrounding yourself with new information and people.

2. *Consequence:* Evaluate the consequences. Honestly ask what worked and what did not so that you can evolve and change.

3. *Corrective action:* Take corrective action. Make new choices and be willing to implement and act on them.

TEND TO YOUR OWN CHARACTER AND INTEGRITY

A distinguished academic interviewed for a professorship at a local university. Faculty and students alike were excited by the possibility of his joining them. The meetings went very well, and the appointment was all but secured. Unfortunately, he then padded his expense report for the trip. This was a minor fraud in the scheme of things, but a red flag in the character department. The plum job went to someone else.

Character, integrity, morality, and ethics are the foundation principles for leadership. They show up in many decisions and choices both large and small. Your character is the set of qualities that defines who you are; your adherence to a moral code guides your daily actions and measures your integrity. A character based on strong integrity builds trust. Others' trust in you gives you your leadership mandate. Loyalty and commitment will follow. Commitment, as we all know, is a cornerstone of productivity and success.

As a leader, you have a responsibility to pass the *New York Times* test every day: if this action showed up on the front page of the *Times*, would it look OK? In increasingly transparent organizations, ethics violations are not worth the risks. Integrity at the core of your character shows up in many ways: Do I live according to legal and social norms? Do I keep promises? Do I live a moral life outside work? Do I avoid gossip, lying, and stealing time? Have I established a code of conduct for my company that I demonstrate through my behaviors?

Integrity and character is somewhat obvious. When leaders have it, others know it; when they don't, others avoid them.

TAKE CARE OF YOURSELF

Leaders who are under incredible scrutiny and pressure have to find ways to renew themselves. Self-care means building resilience by increasing your capacity to respond to adversity and sustaining your energy in the face of inevitable difficulty. As a leader, you need to take care of yourself on many dimensions.

- *Physical:* Nutrition, exercise, sleep, meditation, and healthy living allow you to have the stamina to lead. Physical fatigue leads to poor decision making and a lack of confidence from followers. You do not have to be a world-class athlete, but you need to pay attention to your body's signals and respond to them.

- *Emotional:* Being an optimist, having a good self-image, having a sense of humor, and feeling that you control your demands help you reduce stress. Taking time to renew daily, weekly, or monthly not only increases your energy but sends a signal to others who watch and mimic you. Renewal comes in many ways. We coached one leader to spend regular time at his vacation ranch with his family. Another attended a World Series game with his son. Another made a commitment to not miss his daughter's high school plays, even if it meant ending meetings early and chartering a plane to be home on time. Another had a phone number only family members could access, and any time it rang, he answered it—regardless of whether he was in a meeting. Another had a photography hobby and took wonderful nature pictures. Another went on long bike rides with friends who did not work at his company. Another was active in a local church where parishioners were generally not part of the work organization. Finding your way to renew is important and easy to dismiss as idle time.

- *Social:* As discussed above, leadership is a team event. You need to surround yourself with individuals who are allies and friends. Having colleagues who care for you and for whom you care builds a social network that sustains you. Taking time to connect with your cohorts gives you support when things are difficult. Leaders build relationships of trust with key individuals who support them by caring for them and challenging them from an attitude of affection. When we asked a leader under attack from the press of business how she coped, she said that her 7:30 a.m. call with her team, regardless of where they were in the world, was a source of real support. You need to resist withdrawing into your office to work harder and longer. Be proactive in reaching out to the people that you need, really listening to what they have to offer, and, of course, reciprocating. Appreciate what other people can provide to you.

HAVE PERSONAL ENERGY AND PASSION

Predispositions are our preferences and natural abilities. Passions are our life source and our drive, and they come from our deepest values and needs. When we connect our abilities to our passions we find meaning. Meaning comes when your work results in outcomes you care about, when you work with people you enjoy, and when you help others grow. Help others find meaning. Your ultimate passion is the passion you create in others.

How do you do this? You need to show exceptional commitment and energy. Others around you need to see and feel how passionately you enjoy and care about the work that you do.

As you work on these issues, you care for and invest in yourself. Who you are inside affects who you will be with others. Leaders who care for themselves monitor how they are doing and know when to engage and when to disengage.

Personal proficiency starts from within. As you care for yourself you will be better able to care for others. When a well has a source of living water, it continues to provide fresh water to those who draw from the well. To lead, you need to find ways to replenish and take care of yourself so that you can be a source of living water from those who draw from you.

For real-life stories of leaders who are exceptionally personally proficient, visit our Web site leadership-codebook.com to hear Kate Sweetman on the topic. The premium personal proficiency self-assessment and personal proficiency 360 assessment tools can be accessed there as well.

SEVEN

Ensuring Better Leaders and Leadership

To take action on the leadership code:

1. Establish a clear theory of leadership.

2. Assess leaders.

3. Invest in leaders.

4. Follow up to align organizational practices.

PREVIOUS CHAPTERS DESCRIBE rules for becoming better strategists, executors, talent managers, and human capital developers and for improving personal proficiency. We like the metaphor of rules because having rules enables disciplined action and taking disciplined action helps accomplish desired outcomes while allowing for improvement. Examples of rules that enable action are all around us:

- Rules of the road help you drive more safely.

- Rules of the game let you play better.

- Rules of writing (grammar, spelling, punctuation) allow us to communicate more clearly.

- Rules of order help us run better meetings.

- Rules of evidence are the basis for jurisprudence and guide attorneys and judges.

- Rules of thumb guide practical action.

- Rules of conduct guide how to arbitrate differences.

- Rules of etiquette shape how we behave in social settings.

The leadership code suggests five rules of leadership. We call these rules a *code* because they synthesize a great deal of leadership research about what makes leaders effective. However, in order to be useful, rules not only have to be defined, but be used and lead to action.

So how to act on the rules of leadership we have described? In chapter 1, we proposed that the code is like the architecture of the four food groups. In order to be healthy, we need to eat from all food groups. It's unhealthy to concentrate on just one kind of food just because we like it more than the others or because it is cheaper or easier to get. The code helps us avoid the trap of emphasizing one element of leadership over the others. Good leaders must have knowledge, skills, and perspective in all of the code elements.

In this chapter, we'll explore ideas about how to use all elements of the code together to build better leadership and to be a better leader. Finally, we'll describe what else needs to be in place in addition to the leadership code to optimize quality of leadership.

ESTABLISH A CLEAR THEORY OF LEADERSHIP

As we tried out the ideas in *The Leadership Code*, we identified a variety of exercises with groups of leaders from different companies. One of the most powerful exercises was one we called "Guess My Company." In this exercise, we asked in advance of the class session for the company's leadership competency model. So, in an open enrollment executive development class we might receive competency models representing twenty different companies from all over the world in different industries. For each of these competency models we would take off the name of the company so that it could not be identified.

In advance of the class, we had already posted the twenty competency models on the walls in the room. We did not identify which list belonged to which company. We asked each person to complete two tasks:

- Find your own company's competency model in the midst of the others.

- Identify which competency model belongs to which company.

The results are always the same. Other than by chance, most people cannot pick out their own company's leadership competency model, much less identify those from other companies. In essence, this exercise demonstrated that the leadership competency models of IBM, Tata, and Nokia had far more similarities than differences. The companies were disappointed to discover that their competencies were not nearly as distinctive as they had expected, yet intrigued to find out the common expectations around leadership across companies. But here's the really interesting observation: the exercise also revealed that no one company had a set of leadership competencies that it would consider to be complete—there was always a key set of traits missing from what they had previously believed to be full set for their firm.

Because of the risk of missing a key element in your leadership competency model, we propose a simple test of your existing competency model: map it to the leadership code. We have learned that this exercise is compelling because more often than not, company competency models are unbalanced when compared with the code, often over- or underrepresented in every aspect of the code. Through a few examples, we see how easily this can happen.

Consider the global manufacturing company where we found that eight of their twelve competencies were placed in the leadership code *executor* area and three of the remaining four were in the *personal proficiency* area. If you think about it, this is an easy mistake to make. Leaders in a manufacturing company have a quality and operations mind-set. Since their business depends on great execution, the interviews with senior executives reveal what great leaders do in their organization—they execute. However, effective leaders in manufacturing also need to be good strategists, talent developers, and human capital developers or they will be blindsided at some point. When you also consider that competencies are typically used to guide performance management, development, and succession you realize that most of leadership development in this company was aimed at selecting, developing, and highly compensating people primarily in only one of the critical leadership areas. Effective leaders can specialize in one area for a while but by the time they are in senior executive roles, they need to have strong competencies in all leadership code domains or they create risk for the future of the company. Like eating from just one of the four food groups, by concentrating on only one area, this company's leadership could only remain healthy in the short term.

When we mapped the competency model of a global technology company, the map skewed overwhelmingly to personal proficiency. Again, there's nothing wrong with helping leaders to increase personal proficiency—except when it is done to the exclusion of the other four areas. The logic of the leadership code is that by the time a person becomes a senior executive, all of the domains must be developed. Therefore, any competency model and development plan that does not support building all five leadership code competencies is incomplete.

Embed Competencies with Developmental Depth. After you have built a complete leadership competency model that contains all of the leadership code elements, take a moment to savor the accomplishment. Now ask yourself a simple question: do all leaders do the competencies the same way? Of course not. So, what's different about how leaders at different levels demonstrate each of the competencies? It's clear that the expectations for being a strategist are different for a frontline supervisor and for a senior executive. The senior executive is expected to understand industry dynamics and competitive options and to set a direction for an entire company, business, or function. The supervisor is expected to understand the strategy and its implications for her area and to align her team to that direction. Even the way execution is done is different for those in different stages in their career. Based on these important shifts, we have worked with some organizations to create developmental depth by describing how competencies are done differently as individuals progress through the leadership pipeline. We have already described the logic for doing this in our discussion of the human capital developer in chapter 5—we use the four stages framework.

Figure 7-1 presents an example of how this was done for a large information systems department of a major telecommunications company. In this example, we provide a clear development progression for how to build a key competency for a strategist: "Invite your savviest outsiders inside." Note that even though the competency stays the same, the expectations, knowledge, skills, and perspective shift considerably at each major transition point—from new hire to individual contributor; from

FIGURE 7-1

Inviting outsiders inside

"Invite your savviest outsiders inside"	Learn	Master	Manage/ mentor	Direct/ define
Manage relationships with external sources such as vendors, other companies, professional societies, and universities.	Build and maintain a network of external relationships that add value to the company.	Monitor external relationships to assure needs and expectations of the company are being met.	Tap into personal network of external relationships for ideas on improving the company's IS practices.	Share the company's position on strategic issues to external sources. Represent the company in high-level interaction with external resources. Influences external policy makers to make it easier for the company to conduct business at its locations. Works with global industry leaders in other companies to exchange policies and practices and to set industry standards.

individual contributor to supervisor, manager, or technical idea leader; and finally to senior executive:

Perhaps the most helpful aspect of describing the key development transitions is that it helps the individual leader know what is expected and helps executives and HR specialists to design and manage leadership support practices such as performance management, training and development, and compensation.

By using the leadership code as a guide to your company's theory of leadership and by tailoring the competencies to levels in an organization, you can begin to create a robust and complete theory of leadership.

You should also consider your theory of leadership at a personal level. Ask: What competencies come more readily to you? What do you find easy, energizing, and enjoyable? Then, match your personal predispositions to the requirements of your job today and the job you aspire to tomorrow: Do you have what it takes to meet today's tasks? Are you prepared for the requirements of tomorrow? Find out what jobs you might move into and discover what they will require for you to succeed in those jobs.

Your company's theory of leadership sets standards that guide leadership behavior and outcomes. This theory should clearly define what leaders inside your organization should know and to do meet financial and customer expectations outside your organization.

ASSESS LEADERS

With a shared theory of leadership in place, assessment is the next logical step. Assessment leads to a targeted individual plan that equips each individual to take charge of her own development. The combination of scrimpy assessment and a "build on your strengths" paradigm leads to all kinds of misdirected good intentions. Investing in whatever interests you without a development plan wastes a lot of time and money—use the code instead. In a recent leadership course we taught for a large natural resources company, a few of the leaders had no clue about what kind of development they should target. One person in particular assumed that he was a very adept leader and that the course itself was a waste of his talent. A week or so later, in a conversation with his boss, we learned that this man had several interpersonal weaknesses that jeopardized his career with the organization and that the course was intended to help him improve. This kind of wasted opportunity happens too frequently.

There are simple and high-impact tools available that ensure effective assessment.

Leadership 360s. There are two kinds of 360s—survey and interviews. Both work very well. The intent of the 360 assessments is to give the individual leader feedback about how his level of mastery of the leadership code elements is perceived by himself, his boss, his peers, and his direct reports. When the leader has contact with groups external to the organization such as customers, analysts, suppliers, and consultants, we recommend getting their perceptions as well. Half of the value in the 360 is finding out what other people think of your competencies, the other half of the value is identifying what it means and taking action to improve. The action plan should be tied to creating value for a stakeholder of the leader. We recommend that improvements be described in "so that" results action statements that are reviewed with trusted others. For example, if a leader is going to improve her listening skills based on 360-degree feedback, she might write a statement like one of the following:

"I will improve my listening skills so that I can do a better job with our customers of linking their needs with our products and services."

Or:

"I will improve my listening skills so that the employees on my team perceive that I understand their concerns."

Or:

"I will improve my listening skills so that I connect better with my peers when I am presenting information about what our group is doing."

Behavioral Event Interviews (BEIs). These in–depth interviews explore an individual's career in order to help that individual better understand what experiences have already occurred and what additional experiences are needed for future career aspirations. We like the BEI for many reasons. Chief among them is that they get the participants to do self-reflection about what they like and what they don't like. As leaders progress in their career, they need to have a variety of experiences that allow them to guide the organization as conditions change. Typical experiences include turning around a troubled team, involvement in a merger or acquisition, responsibility for profit and loss of a small business, responsibility for profit and loss for a larger business, a foreign culture experience, a staff experience, and so on. The BEI is a strong foundation for building a targeted development plan.

Psychometric Assessments. The development, assessment, evaluation, and selection of leaders and leadership involve a complex mixture of psychological tests and tools that have been in use for decades with strong results. Every effort to reduce guesswork, refine decision making, and provide empirical explanations on a variety of scales can enhance an organization's efforts at building a team of leaders. Psychometric assessment tools are in wide use in government, military, private-sector, and academic settings.

As far back as the 1970s, the U.S. Forest Service was selective in whom it allowed on teams going into the wilderness to fight dangerous forest fires because of fears that the behavior of individuals who were not team oriented might not be appropriate to meet the challenges encountered in remote areas where medical care is not available.

The military has long employed psychological tools for selection. These assessments are used to help select members of special units, as well as to develop officers for effective performance at progressively higher levels of leadership.

Private-sector firms are increasingly using these assessments. One of the most visible examples is the National Football League's (NFL) evaluation of player draft prospects. Our colleagues at Human Resource Tactics (HRT) use their psychological assessment tools to assist roughly half of the NFL clubs in making decisions about which players to draft, with literally millions of dollars—and reputations—at stake every year. The optimum combination of psycho-logical characteristics varies by position on the football field. Drawing on years of work and careful measurement and analysis, HRT was able to develop tests that measure the best combination of psychological traits for each posi-tion. These metrics are strong predictors of (1) on-the-field NFL performance and (2) the ability to avoid trouble off the field. Corporations use these psychometric tools for similar selection and assessment uses.

At a personal level, become a feedback junkie. Take fre-quent and honest looks in the leadership mirror. Review frequently how you performed in a given situation, what you did well, and what you did poorly. Learn to solicit feedback, listen to it, sift it, see patterns in it, and act on it. Try to avoid making the same mistake over and over again as you develop as a leader. We have been privileged to coach leaders who have learned to set strategies, ensure accountabilities, engage others, and share decision making even when they were not predisposed to do so. They did so by knowing what they needed to do to improve and then by making personal commitments to improve.

INVEST IN LEADERS

Leadership competencies represent the skills, knowledge, and perspective leaders must have to be effective as they transition through the leadership pipeline. Once these competencies are clarified, leadership practices can be aligned in order to build quality of leadership as a sustainable organization capability. In a 2006 study of "Leaders Who Develop Leaders: Establishing the Foundations of Effective Leader-Led Development," the Learning and Development Roundtable (a subset of the Corporate Executive Board) asked senior learning executives to rate the most powerful drivers for building leadership bench strength. In order of priority, the top three areas are:

1. Coaching provided by the leader's direct manager

2. Job rotations and assignments

3. Action learning[1]

Some comments on each of these high-impact approaches frames the opportunity to develop leaders through these areas:

Coaching Provided by the Leader's Direct Manager. It's hard to overstate the importance of this simple and powerful revelation—leaders are better equipped to contribute when they can talk to their boss about what high performance looks like in the current job. We find that any initiative aimed at getting people to talk to one another about how they can remain or become high performers is high impact. There are several reasons why managers don't like to talk to their direct reports about their careers. First, they often don't have a shared language (like the leadership code) to discuss performance. Second, they don't want to get into a conversation about specific jobs that may or may not be available in the future, even if the direct report does a great job in his current role. Third, at least some managers try to avoid conflict when performance is not in line, so they just don't have the conversation. To make matters worse, the direct report often has his reasons for avoiding conversations about performance. Like the manager, the direct report often lacks a language or framework for thinking about development. Second, direct reports may want to get out of their manager's team in order to develop in an alternate area but are concerned about the repercussions of asking for a transfer. Finally, like the managers, some direct reports just don't like conflict, so avoid the discussion.

Combining these reasons for avoiding coaching by the leader's direct manager with the importance of doing it, we have to find ways to make these coaching discussions occur. The 2006 Conference Executive Board study cited above describes several roles that the direct manager can play to fulfill this responsibility. When one or more of these roles are played effectively, the direct manager can have a significant impact on performance:

- *Performance adviser:* Performance advisers coach direct reports to the right answers by asking questions, not by telling them how to do things. Performance advisers tend to focus on building direct reports' strengths rather than address their weaknesses.

- *Relationship broker:* Relationship brokers assist direct reports to build the *right* relationships rather than building more relationships—it's about quality, not quantity, of relationships. They also leverage their influence by helping their reports navigate their networks across the organization.

- *Experience broker and experience optimizer:* Experience brokers create connections between critical career experiences and career advancement. They also help the direct report "mine" the current job for development value. Experience optimizers ensure that their reports take the time to reflect and learn from their experiences as well as to act and apply what they learn to their job.

- *Career champion:* The best senior leaders act as visible, active champions for the long-term potential of rising leaders and create linkages between development and advancement requirements.[2]

Job Rotation and Assignment. There's an old saying in real estate that the three most important factors for success are "location, location, location." In leadership development the three most important factors for success are "job assignment, job assignment, job assignment." Over the last few years, we have been fortunate to partner with Hewitt, the large HR consultancy on the "Top Companies for Leaders" (TCFL) study published by *Fortune* magazine every other year. Through this study, we have learned some key differences between what the best companies do in leadership compared with everyone else. One difference is that top companies are more likely than others to identify high potentials and then label them corporate property. Corporate property means that these targeted people are no longer under the "control" of a business, function, or geography. Their careers are managed by corporate. This is important because once a person establishes a reputation as a high performer, departments are reluctant to let that person leave the area. Corporate property individuals belong to the entire company and are moved around accordingly. The intent is to move high-potential leaders through a variety of developmental experiences across company lines to test them and to provide them with the experience set they will need to be effective senior leaders.

It's very clear that the best leaders are those who get these broad and deep experiences that they can draw on to be effective in their current and future jobs—these job rotation experiences equip them to be effective strategists, executors, human capital developers, and talent managers while sustaining their personal proficiency. A framework like the leadership code guides those helping to develop leaders in offering these developing leaders job assignments that build the required perspectives in each code element. So, a high-potential leader gets assessed through a 360, a BEI, and a battery of psychometric tests to identify targeted development needs. An individual action plan is identified that delineates specific areas for improvement to keep the high-potential leader on the leadership path. Both the individual and her direct manager talk as well. For example, a turnaround situation is likely to build strategy, execution, and talent manager skills. A stint in human resources provides a budding technical star (like an engineer or a chemist) the opportunity to do some human capital planning. A job rotation to a leadership job in a foreign country definitely pushes the boundaries of personal proficiency and talent manager experiences.

Action Learning. Action learning is a powerful development tool because it shifts the emphasis from talking about leadership to doing leadership. The best action learning is done within the sweet spot of what the business needs and what the leader needs to develop. A few years ago IBM initiated an action-learning approach that involved identifying chronic business problems and then pulling teams from across the world together to solve the problem in eight, ten, or twelve weeks. This is a high-impact approach for several reasons. First, a chronic business problem usually gets resolved, so the action learning is measurably helpful. Second, leaders involved in the action learning are educated about problem solving, team building and other people, organization, and technical content as they relate to a specific business problem. Third, IBM is interested in both speed of change and collaboration. The process of pulling the right people together to solve a problem from across the globe is collaborative, and giving eight-, ten-, or twelve-week time frames to solve the problem promotes speed. So, participants gain individual competence and the organization reinforces key capabilities of speed and collaboration.

Done right, action learning is a powerful vehicle for high-impact development. As designers of action learning prepare action-learning projects, a huge benefit is gained by matching action-learning projects to targeted individual leader development needs. For example, if an individual's development plan suggests that he needs better financial grounding before starting execution, a project can be found or tweaked where this person can test his skills in this area.

At a personal level, invest in yourself. Some of this may be behind-the-scenes learning where you read articles or books on topics in which you know you are weak, but other personal investment may come from taking on difficult assignments that place you in a position to learn. As a leader, you probably should develop your own "half-life of leadership" index, which indicates when 50 percent of what you know and do as a leader is out of date. In the information and economy age, we have found this time frame is getting increasingly shorter as what you did to become a leader will not sustain you in being a future leader.

FOLLOW UP TO ALIGN ORGANIZATIONAL PRACTICES

In order to sustain a leadership process over time, there must be follow-up to ensure that organization practices, especially HR practices, are aligned for success. These practices must be aligned not only to the business strategy but also to each other.

Compensation. In a global financial services company, we correlated executive bonuses with 360 scores. To our horror, we discovered that 360s were inversely correlated to size of bonus—executives with the lowest 360s got the highest bonus. This is a powerful example of misalignment. In leadership theory and assessment and investment practices, leaders were told that they are judged not just on results but on how they create value to their stakeholders and "it's not just about getting results but how you get results." On the compensation side, none of that mattered; it was all about delivering results. Execution was king. Talent managers, human capital developers, and strategists could jump in the lake. No one was even looking at these kinds of contributions at executive bonus time. In this particular example, even after we showed the data to senior executives, no one seemed to care. About a year later, regulators had to step in for a series of leadership misconduct problems, several senior executives lost their jobs, and a new CEO sponsored a new, more aligned process.

When you look at your firm's compensation system, start with the standards by which people are paid. Examine these standards. Do they reflect customer expectations? Do they capture your organization's strategy? If someone were to look at the behaviors and outcomes you and your employees are accountable for, would they be able to identify key success factors for your firm? Further ask if the compensation system differentiates high and low performers? When people meet standards, do good things happen; and when people miss standards, do bad things happen? We have learned that compensation systems may not lead change, but they often sustain it in your organization.

Succession. Our hint for succession is to look broadly rather than narrowly at succession. Many companies don't pick a large enough pool of candidates to consider for high-impact jobs and often find themselves shortchanged when it's time for succession. Perhaps the simplest measure of leadership bench strength is the number of "ready candidates" for top executive and critical jobs. Critical jobs are the few wealth-producing jobs that are the life's blood of every firm and were discussed in chapter 5—these are the high-impact jobs. Having too many candidates ready for a top job is a rare situation because most companies can't afford the time and energy to create the conditions necessary for this to occur. It's also frustrating for candidates if there is too much competition and not enough job opportunity. The reverse case is more often true—not enough candidates to fill senior and critical jobs when they are needed. Good succession planning is finding the zone between too many and too few candidates for important roles.

Having succession-ready candidates at the right time involves coordination across important practices such as recruiting, performance management, job assignment, training and development, and compensation. Those involved in succession planning can use the developmental depth logic and the assessment information described in chapter 5 to plan job assignments that build experiences across the leadership code elements. It's essential that the succession-planning process ensures that candidates have the right set of experiences so that they can fill jobs with the right kind of leadership code experiences in their background.

Training and Development. Those involved in classroom-based training and development must ensure that the content of leadership development covers all of the leadership code elements. It's not surprising to see bias in training and development curriculums when the leadership competency models are incomplete and biased only to selected leadership code pieces. To develop effective leaders requires training in all elements of the leadership code and delivering content relevant to each stage in the leadership pipeline. As we have pointed out elsewhere, senior executives and supervisors have the same elements of the code to learn but have completely different expectations and knowledge, skills, and perspectives for how to deliver.

Shared frameworks, theories, and models taught in classroom training to different leadership levels are very effective. So, if your company has a point of view on how to increase engagement—the role of the talent manager—with employees, it's important that leaders at different levels are using the common language and tools. Otherwise, it's impossible to get critical mass and see real change as a result of the training investment. In the engagement example, the role of the senior executive is to support the philosophy of employee engagement, sponsor the consistent practice of engagement, and reward leaders who deliver high levels of employee engagement. On the front end of the pipeline, the role of the technical idea leader or supervisor is to measure engagement on the team, understand the specific circumstances of particular employees, and take action to improve the situation on the team. Training investments should be aimed at building all code elements combined with structured experiences and action learning relevant to level in the leadership hierarchy.

FOR THE ORGANIZATION, the net effect of these follow-up systems is to ensure that leadership is less about the individual leader and more about the capability of leadership in the organization. A talented individual may rise to the occasion and lead well, but when the systems are in place to produce a flow of future leaders, both the organization and you are successful.

As an individual, you should be proactive in taking advantage of these organization systems. If you believe that your compensation system does not reflect what you should be doing and delivering, challenge and change it. Self-select for assignments where you will learn and grow. Sign up for training courses where you will be exposed to new ideas. You are your own career manager and need to invest wisely in yourself.

WHAT ELSE IS NEEDED? LEADERSHIP BRAND

When we first described the leadership code, we said it is a synthesis of what it takes to be an effective leader. According to the thought leaders we interviewed, it also explains about 60 to 70 percent of the leadership puzzle. So, what's the other 30 to 40 percent?

To explain the other 30 to 40 percent, think of giving Richard Branson, CEO of Virgin Airlines, and Jeff Immelt, CEO of GE, a leadership code 360. We bet that both would score very high on the 360. Both are strong strategists; they both know how to execute and to get their ideas implemented by others; they are both high in personal proficiency; both are talent developers; and both are concerned about the next generation of talent and act as human capital developers. So, according to our 360, they are both effective leaders. They have the code competencies. But they are also very different.

From a personal style perspective, Immelt wears his hair short and often wears a suit and tie, while we're not sure if we've ever seen the shaggy-haired Branson in a suit—much less a tie. Branson is playful while Immelt tends to come across as more conservative and businesslike. Immelt speaks in a more formal manner in public, whereas Branson tends to use "colorful" language to make his points. Branson seems somewhat "touchy-feely," while Immelt seems a tad more aloof. So, they have some real differences in style.

In our earlier book, *Leadership Brand*, we focused on these unique aspects of leadership.[3] Our simple formula is that leadership brand comprises:

$$\text{Leadership Code} \times \text{Leadership Differentiators} = \text{Leadership Brand}$$

The graphic in figure 7-2 illustrates this formula.

The leadership differentiators come from the firm's identity or *firm brand*. This firm brand is the way the company wants to be described by its target customers. Typically the firm brand descriptors are the firm's customer value proposition along with how the company

FIGURE 7-2

Effective leadership brand

As leaders at all levels of the company learn how to master both the basic skills of leadership and the unique essence of your leadership brand, they will establish sustainable value.

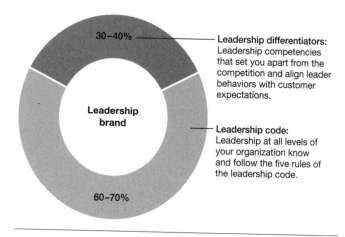

30–40% — Leadership differentiators: Leadership competencies that set you apart from the competition and align leader behaviors with customer expectations.

Leadership brand

Leadership code: Leadership at all levels of your organization know and follow the five rules of the leadership code.

60–70%

wants its target customers to experience that value proposition. Southwest Airlines' value proposition is low price. However, Southwest also wants its customers to experience the low price value proposition in a different way than other low price competitors—it wants Southwest customers to see it also as "on time" and "fun." These three words—*low price, on time,* and *fun*—are Southwest's firm brand identity in the minds of its best customers.

The next step is to translate these firm brand descriptors into *leadership differentiators*—the unique leadership competencies that make the firm brand real to the customers whenever they interact with any employee of the firm. These leadership differentiators are always outside-in; they bring the customer mind-set to the table. In the Southwest Airlines example, the best Southwest Airlines leaders make sure that whenever a customer flies on a Southwest flight, that customer has a fun experience. This is done through selecting the right flight attendants, rewarding people in any job who improvise to find ways to have fun with customers in a way the customer enjoys, and celebrating successes. As a result of the culture, which is reinforced by leaders at every level, most customers find flying on Southwest to be a unique experience that they quite enjoy—even if they did not get a first-class seat or a free meal.

Let's revisit Immelt and Branson now. Jeff Immelt personifies GE's firm identity. He is a role model to other GE leaders about how the firm should be seen by outside stakeholders. GE's firm identity is about organic growth and innovation with a lot of measurement and accountability going on. Virgin's firm identity is about fun, irreverence, and challenging the status quo; and that's exactly what Richard Branson is constantly doing. He owns property on an island and seems to enjoy the high life in ways that the rest of us can only dream of. He personifies the leadership style of the Virgin brand.

When GE or Virgin or Southwest can develop leaders at every level who have their own style that fits within the context of the differing firm identities, the company has a leadership brand that is appreciated by customers and employees and rewarded by financial markets as an envied capability. Assessment 7-1 provides a brief exercise for you to evaluate the effectiveness of your own leadership brand.

At a personal level, Tom Peters, Libby Sartain, and others have suggested that you are your own brand.[4] You need to define and become the leader you want to become. You need to create personal differentiators that distinguish you from others. By mastering the code and developing differentiators you establish your identity and personal brand.

It's not about leadership code versus leadership differentiators. It's about building leaders who have both. Leaders need to have the leadership code building blocks to be effective leaders, and they need to know how their organization is unique in how it ensures a desired customer connection. It's a big job to get all of this done. Your company and your leaders need you to get working.

ASSESSMENT 7-1

Leadership brand assessment

The following questions assess the extent to which your organization has shaped a leadership brand. The leadership brand builds on the leadership code and aligns the behaviors of your leaders with customer expectations. You can also take a comprehensive assessment online at www.leadershipcodebook.com.

Scale: 1 = Low ◄ - - ► 10 = High

We have articulated a clear business case about why we should make investments in leadership.	1 2 3 4 5 6 7 8 9 10
Our senior executives devote time, resources and their personal attention to building leaders at every level.	1 2 3 4 5 6 7 8 9 10
We have created a unique logic for what our leaders should be known for that is widely understood and accepted.	1 2 3 4 5 6 7 8 9 10
We have an explicit process to connect leadership behaviors to customer expectations.	1 2 3 4 5 6 7 8 9 10
Our organization identifies gaps in the knowledge, experiences, and perspectives of our next generation of leaders at key stages in their development.	1 2 3 4 5 6 7 8 9 10
Leaders at every level have an individual development plan that focuses them on building the competencies they will need for future success.	1 2 3 4 5 6 7 8 9 10
Our diverse leadership development practices integrate and support each other (e.g. job assignments, 360s, succession, performance management, compensation, training).	1 2 3 4 5 6 7 8 9 10
Our leadership practices include the perspectives of external stakeholders (e.g. customers, investors, analysts).	1 2 3 4 5 6 7 8 9 10
We measure the business impact of our leadership investments (beyond enjoying training programs).	1 2 3 4 5 6 7 8 9 10
The views of external stakeholders (e.g. analysts, media, and community) impact the way we invest in and develop leaders.	1 2 3 4 5 6 7 8 9 10

Scoring: Total:_____

Over 90 = *Pat yourself on the back—and buy more of your company's stock.*

80–89 = *You are already a leadership brand company.*

60–79 = *You should pick one or more areas where you can improve your leadership capability efforts.*

Under 60 = *Start by building the fundamentals of leadership. You are likely focusing too much effort on individual development and not enough on leadership development as an organization capability.*

Norm Smallwood provides the closing chapter on this book and a discussion of leadership brand on our site www.leadershipcodebook.com. Please view his video, and take the full-length leadership code assessment (self- or 360) if you have not done so already.

Notes

Chapter One

1. Competency theorists include: Richard E. Boyatzis. *The Competent Manager: A Model for Effective Performance* (New York: Wiley, 1982); Lyle M. Spencer and Signe M. Spencer, *Competence at Work: Models for Superior Performance* (New York: Wiley. 1993).

2. Results-focused theorists include: Jack Zenger, Joe Folkman, Bob Eichinger, and Mike Lombando.

3. These generous thought leaders are named and thanked in the acknowledgments.

4. Personal correspondence with Jack Zenger. Cited with permission.

5. Matthieu Ricard, *Happiness: A Guide to Developing Life's Most Important Skill*, trans. Jesse Browner (New York: Little, Brown, 2006), 5.

Chapter Four

1. All quotations of leaders are from interviews by the authors from 2000 to 2008.

2. http://www.catalyst.org/publication/82/the-bottom-line-connecting-corporate-performance-and-gender-diversity

184 Notes

3. Wendy Ulrich, *Identification and Referral of Depressed Secondary School Students* (PhD diss., University of Michigan, 1989).

4. Martin Seligman, *Authentic Happiness: Using the New Positive Psychology to Realize Your Potential For Lasting Fulfillment* (New York, Free Press 2004).

5. Adrian Gostick and Chester Elton, *The Carrot Principle: How the Best Managers Use Recognition to Engage Their Employees, Retain Talent, and Drive Performance* (New York: Free Press, 2007).

Chapter Five

1. Gene W. Dalton and Paul H. Thompson, *Novations: Strategies for Career Development* (Glenview, IL: Scott, Foresman and Company, 1986).

2. Beverly L. Kaye and Sharon Jordan-Evans, *Love 'Em or Lose 'Em: Getting Good People to Stay* (San Francisco: Berrett-Koehler, 2005).

Chapter Six

1. Martin Seligman, *Authentic Happiness: Using the New Positive Psychology to Realize Your Potential For Lasting Fulfillment* (New York, Free Press 2004).

2. M. Lombardo and R. Eichinger, *The Leadership Architect Norms and Validity Report* (Minneapolis: Lominger Limited, Inc., 2003); M. M. Lombardo and R. W. Eichinger, "High Potentials as High Learners," *Human Resource Management* 39, no. 4 (2000): 321–330.

Chapter Seven

1. "Leaders Who Develop Leaders: Establishing the Foundations of Effective Leader-Led Development," study by the

Learning and Development Roundtable, 2006, http://hr.insight.
executiveboard.com/ArticleSummary.aspx?practice=29f4f39b-d1
1e-4c80-b249-ff6fdaaa3827&article=f3cf1c1a-040b-4673-bf74-
3c7f999d9e74.

   2. Ibid.

   3. Dave Ulrich and Norm Smallwood, *Leadership Brand:
Developing Customer-Focused Leaders to Drive Performance And
Build Lasting Value* (Boston: Harvard Business School Press,
2007).

   4. See, for example, Tom Peters "The Brand Called You,"
Fast Company, August 1997, 83; Mark Schumann and Libby
Sartain, *Brand from the Inside: Eight Essentials to Emotionally Connect Your Employees to Your Business* (Hoboken, NJ: John Wiley &
Sons, 2006).

About the Authors

Dave Ulrich is Professor of Business Administration at the University of Michigan and a partner at The RBL Group, a consulting firm focused on helping organizations and leaders deliver value. He has developed ideas with impact around leadership, organization, and HR. He has published over one hundred articles and book chapters and fifteen books, including *The HR Value Proposition* (with Wayne Brockbank), *Why the Bottom Line Isn't: How to Build Value Through People and Organizations* (with Norm Smallwood), *The HR Scorecard: Linking People, Strategy, and Performance* (with Brian Becker and Mark Huselid), *Results-Based Leadership: How Leaders Build the Business and Improve the Bottom Line* (with Jack Zenger and Norm Smallwood), *Human Resource Champions: The Next Agenda for Adding Value and Delivering Results,* and *The Boundaryless Organization: Breaking the Chains of Organization Structure* (with Ron Ashkenas, Steve Kerr, and Todd Jick).

Dave was the editor of *Human Resource Management Journal* (1990–1999) and served on the editorial board of four other journals. He is on the board of directors for Herman Miller, is a Fellow in the National Academy of Human Resources, and is Cofounder of the Michigan Human Resource Partnership. He has a number of lifetime achievement awards, was ranked the number-one most influential person in HR by *HR Magazine,* and was named by *Fast Company* as one of the ten most innovative and creative thinkers of 2005. He has consulted and done research with over half of the *Fortune* 200. Dave can be reached at dou@umich.edu.

Norm Smallwood is a recognized authority in developing businesses and their leaders to deliver results and increase value. His current work relates to increasing business value by building organization, strategic HR, and leadership capabilities that measurably impact market value. He is cofounder (with Dave Ulrich) of The RBL Group, a firm of well-known and broadly experienced management educators and consultants. In 2005 and 2006, The RBL Group was ranked as the number-one leadership development firm in the world by Leadership Excellence. He is coauthor of five other books, including *Real-Time Strategy: Improvising Team-Based Planning for a Fast-Changing World* (with Lee Tom Perry and Randall G. Stott),

Results-Based Leadership: How Leaders Build the Business and Improve the Bottom Line (with Dave Ulrich and Jack Zenger), and *Why the Bottom Line Isn't: How to Build Value Through People and Organizations* (with Dave Ulrich).

Norm has contributed chapters to multiple books, and has published more than fifty articles in leading journals and newspapers, including two *Harvard Business Review* articles: "Capitalize Your Capabilities" (June 2004) and "Building a Leadership Brand" (July 2007). He was selected as one of the top 100 Voices in Leadership by *Executive Excellence* magazine in February 2005. Norm can be reached at nsmallwood@rbl.net

Kate Sweetman has worked intensively in leadership development with major global corporations for almost twenty years, with a special emphasis on creative change efforts that link the individual leader's efforts to the larger leadership needs of the organization and the bottom line. Kate and her leadership development team have been honored for delivering exceptional, measurable results to the bottom line by the American Society of Trainers and Developers. In addition to her consulting work, she was an editor at *Harvard Business Review,* acquiring and editing articles by top business executives, academics, and consultants around the world on the topics of leadership, organizational change, organizational design, teamwork, and social enterprise. She has also contributed numerous articles to other publications, including *Sloan Management Review.* She has also taught in the Management Communications Course at Harvard Business School.

In addition to her general work in leadership, Kate also focuses on the specific leadership challenges facing women in becoming leaders in the corporate arena as well as in the world of social enterprise. Kate is a graduate of Yale University and Harvard Business School. Kate is a principal in Leadership at The RBL Group and can be reached at ksweetman@rbl.net.